Blinds, Curtains & Cushions

Design and make stylish treatments for your home

Blinds, Curtains & Cushions

Design and make stylish treatments for your home

CATHERINE MERRICK & REBECCA DAY

Edited by Liselle Barnsley

MERRICK & DAY

Blinds, Curtains & Cushions

For Father, who solved our problems
before we even knew we had them.

Throughout the course of writing this book, we have been helped by many people; in particular, we would like to thank:
Liselle Barnsley, Mike & Jessica Beard, Paul & Zoë Eaton, Jane Read, Judy Stevens, Mrs & Mrs R Borrill, Mr & Mrs M Ferron, Mr & Mrs M Hodgkinson, Mr & Mrs C Jago, Mrs A Mollo, Mrs G Peckitt, Mr & Mrs C Travers, all the staff at Merrick & Day and our families.

The rights of Catherine Merrick and Rebecca Day to be identified as the authors of this work have been asserted by them in accordance with the Copyright Designs and Patent Act 1988.

A CIP record for this book is available from the British Library.

The publishers have made every effort to ensure that all the instructions and measurements given in this publication are accurate and safe, but they cannot accept liability for any resulting injury, damage or loss to either person or property whether direct or consequential and howsoever arising.

The measurements in this publication are approximate as are the conversions of measurements from metric to Imperial.

ISBN 0-9535267-5-5

Printed and bound in China by Leo Paper Products Limited 2006

Editor: Liselle Barnsley, Tailored Marketing Solutions Limited
Graphic design: Paul Eaton, Redback Visual
Photography: see picture credits, page 144
Diagrams: Jessica Beard & Suzanne Kettle

Merrick & Day
Redbourne Hall, Redbourne, Gainsborough, Lincolnshire DN21 4JG, UK
Telephone: 08707 570980 Facsimile: 08707 570985
Email: sales@merrick-day.com Website: www.merrick-day.com

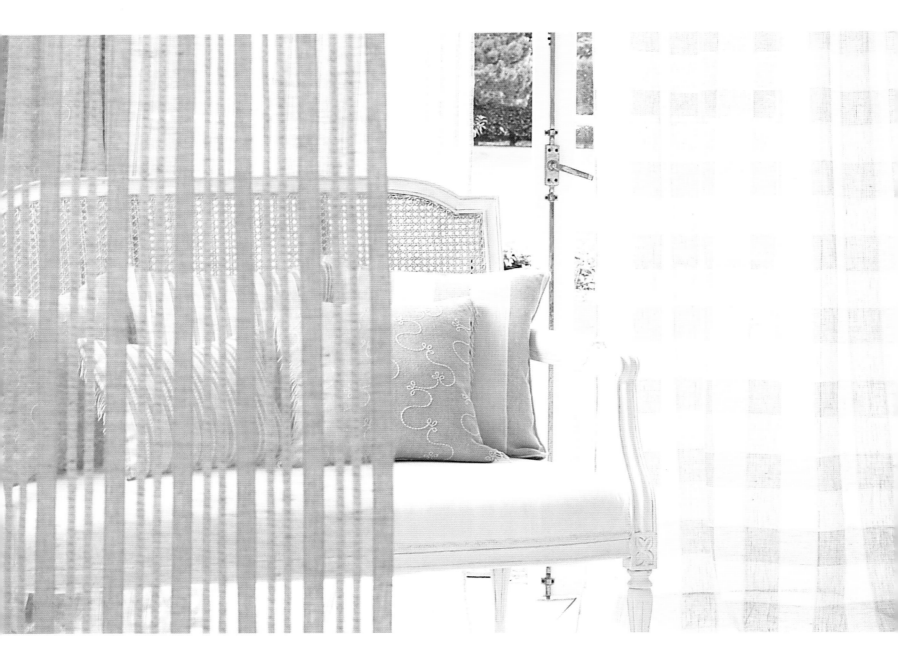

Introduction

This is a book about the blinds, curtains and cushions used in our homes today.

In these pages you will find inspiring pictures, combined with practical advice and clear make-up instructions, designed to help you choose and make your soft furnishing treatments with confidence.

Three sections explain blinds, curtains and cushions with clarity and detail; from wooden Venetian blinds to fabric Roman blinds, sheer curtains to eyelet-headed ones, plain to panelled cushions.

Each section also includes essential information about measuring and estimating as well as step-by-step projects to suit every level of expertise. Practical hints and tips, direct from our workroom, will help you to achieve a professional finish every time.

Whether you want to make stunning Roman blinds, emphasise a view with curtains, or accessorise your room with cushions, you will find a wealth of information and guidance in *Blinds, Curtains and Cushions*.

Catherine and Rebecca, Redbourne, January 2006

Blinds

"Blinds are a streamlined window treatment"

Blinds

For those of us who want to enjoy the light coming into our homes and maximise the space around our windows, blinds are a good choice.

Blinds were the earliest form of window coverings. Hanging cloths and wooden slats were traditionally used to hinder vision, block out light and provide privacy. Today blinds are still appealing to people for the same reasons as they did hundreds of years ago.

Available in a huge variety of attractive styles, blinds can fit seamlessly into modern or traditional interiors. Blind style options have never been more varied and interesting, with different materials and lifting mechanisms available.

To ensure that you are not bewildered by the extensive choices available we are going to clearly describe the different types of blinds and highlight the key differences between them, so that you can be confident about your choice and enjoy living with your blinds.

Left A series of opaque Roman blinds on a wide window; the opaque fabric disguises an unwanted view.

An easy way to categorise blinds is to describe them as hard or soft. Hard blinds are made out of wooden or aluminium slats, such as Venetian blinds, or woodweave fabrics, such as pinoleum.

Soft blinds are made of fabric. For roller blinds the fabric is usually stiffened; for roll-up and Roman styles the fabric is left untreated, with one or more battens producing the distinctive final forms.

Blinds work well in the majority of rooms. Whether your style is urban, country, traditional or modern, there are blinds to suit your own personal style as well as your budget.

Requiring little or no space around the window, blinds can be fitted either inside or outside the recess. Fitting outside the recess can make your windows appear larger and maximise the light.

Blinds are ideal where space is limited at one or both sides of the window, or if there is a radiator or sink directly below. Blinds are also a neat solution for bay windows as they can be fitted into each angle.

When purchasing blinds you can choose bespoke or ready-made, or if you have the inclination as well as the time and patience you can make soft blinds yourself by following our step-by-step instructions.

Left Woodweave Roman blinds.
Right Fabric Roman blinds.

"Blinds are a practical choice for kitchen windows"

Venetian blinds

Made from narrow overlapping slats, linked with cords or woven ladder tapes, the slats can be angled to filter light.

First used in Europe in the late 18th century, Venetian blinds were introduced via Venice, although it is thought that they actually originated from Persia.

One theory is that the Persians had seen how the fronds of the palm trees filtered light and air and that they copied this idea to make blinds for their homes.

A popular choice for conservatories, Venetian blinds are extremely suitable for all living and working spaces.

Left Venetian blinds fitted inside window reveals are softened with curtains hung from fabric-covered laths.

With their vertical structure and clean lines Venetian blinds work well in unfussy contemporary interiors, but they are surprisingly versatile and also suit traditional settings.

For modern urban living, choose Venetian blinds with aluminium slats to block out an unwanted view. Alternatively, to bring some visual warmth into a room, use wooden or painted slats.

In more traditional living spaces wooden Venetian blinds combine well with curtains. Light-coloured narrow wooden slats can look summery when teamed with pretty floral unlined curtains hung from slim poles, or for a more comfortable feel combine larger wooden slats with lined or interlined curtains.

In kitchens and bathrooms, plastic, wood-effect and aluminium slats work particularly well as they are not affected by the extra moisture in the air. Aluminium slats can also be perforated to provide sun-screening protection without blocking a view.

Right A strongly contrasting ladder tape is a striking feature on this blind.

"Venetian blinds suit modern or traditional interiors"

Tilting the slats allows many variations or shades of light, ranging from near darkness through to almost full daylight.

The slats can be set at an angle that will meet every requirement. Most blinds are dual-control and have a cord to raise and lower the blind and a cord or wand to tilt the slats.

Set in the horizontal position, the slats will allow both air and light to travel into the room. If you prefer subdued light and no draughts then angle the slats up towards the ceiling. However, to obtain brighter light and greater airflow, then angle the slats downwards. For total privacy, just overlap the slats.

It's worth noting that long or floor-length blinds can be quite bulky when raised and stacked up. If you are intending to regularly raise your blinds and keep them in the raised position, then make sure you have enough headroom to accommodate the stack.

When blinds are permanently left down then regular dusting with a feather duster or a slat-cleaning brush will be required.

"No other blind controls the light as well as a Venetian blind"

The slats come in a variety of widths. Micro blinds have aluminium, plastic or wood-effect slats of 15mm (⅝in) width. Mini blinds can also be made from wood and have slats of 25mm (1in). Regular Venetian blinds can be made from any of the above materials and the slats are usually 50mm (2in) wide.

The maximum widths of blinds will vary depending on the slat material you choose. The maximum width for wooden blinds will be approximately 140 to 200cm (55–79in). Aluminium and plastic can be found up to 300cm (118in) wide, so do bear in mind the width of your windows when you are choosing a Venetian blind.

If your windows are particularly wide, then consider hanging two or more blinds side by side.

Venetian blinds can be custom-made or ready-made. It is possible to alter some ready-made blinds to make them fit your windows. You can reduce the width of aluminium, plastic or wood-effect blinds by clipping them at each side with a slat cutter. It is not generally recommended that you alter wooden blinds as they are prone to splitting. The length of ready-made blinds can sometimes be decreased by removing the lower slats.

Vertical louvre blinds

Vertical louvre blinds have slats which close and angle in a similar way to Venetian blinds, but each slat hangs vertically from the headrail.

Vertical louvre blinds are more like curtains in that they are drawn to the centre and pulled back to the side. However, because they are made from a series of slats they are also akin to Venetian blinds.

Vertical louvre blinds offer effective sun protection as they usually hang from ceiling to floor. They are extremely practical and minimalist and very popular in offices.

Vertical slats, sometimes called vanes, are suspended from a headrail with hooks that rotate. The slat bottoms are linked by a continuous chain and weighted to hang straight. Slats are generally available in two widths, 89mm (3½in) and 127mm (5in). When fitting in a recess make sure the depth is 12mm (½in) wider than the slat to allow the blind to be operated.

Each vertical blind comes with two sets of controls – a control cord that draws the slats closed, like curtains, and a chain that angles the slats to control the light.

Vertical louvre blinds are usually custom-made rather than ready-made.

When buying custom-made blinds you can specify whether you want the blinds to close into a left-hand or right-hand stack, a split draw or even a centre stack.

There is a huge range of materials available for the slats, from stiffened fabric to wood and aluminium, in addition to a wide variety of colours. By choosing one colour you can create a dramatic look with a solid block of colour. Alternatively you can mix two or more colours for a more individual look.

"Vertical louvre blinds are a functional solution for wide, full-length windows"

Sliding panels

Inspired by Japanese paper screens, these delicate panels are a sleek and modern window treatment.

Sliding panels are halfway between blinds and curtains. Although classed as blinds because they consist of flat panels, they are drawn open and closed like curtains.

Full-length panels, weighted at the bottom and hung vertically from slim tracks, are designed to stack behind each other to produce a subtle layering effect. They work well on wide windows.

The panels are not linked at the bottom, which can mean they are not as robust or practical as vertical louvre blinds.

As they look good from both sides the panels are suitable as room dividers where you can separate off sections with the screens.

The operation of sliding panels can be very flexible. Panels can either be linked at the top or used individually. If the panels are not linked then the panels can be positioned individually.

If your panels are linked to each other you can pull the leading edge by a draw rod or use a cord fitted at the side. Usually stacked back in pairs, you can also choose to stack the panels to the right, left or the centre.

Panels are usually around 60cm (24in) wide and overlap by approximately 10cm (4in) when closed. Sliding panel systems are available from two panels on a two-track system up to nine panels on a five-track system.

Sliding panels are usually custom-made or bought ready-made. It is possible to buy panel tracks from specialist manufacturers and make your own.

"Sliding panels work well in calm, contemporary interiors"

Pinoleum blinds

Traditionally made from fine pine strips sewn together with spaced thread, pinoleum blinds offer shading and effective temperature control.

The word pinoleum is originally derived from the thin strips of cut pine which are interwoven with cotton yarn to form a fabric.

Woven pinoleum is a light pine colour which will darken naturally in sunlight. It can be made into roll-up and Roman blinds up to 2 metres (79in) in width.

These blinds can be hand-cut to ensure a perfect finish and shape for any window; the edges are then bound with cotton tape. A strongly contrasting coloured binding can look smart.

The weaving gives the blind an attractive effect as the narrow gaps between the reeds allow 'through vision' while offering elegant shading to the room.

Pinoleum binds are seen most often in conservatories where they provide dual protection against the sun by insulating against the heat yet still allowing soft, dappled light to filter through. Custom-made blinds can be made to perfectly fit awkward roof windows.

Pinoleum and woodweave blinds complement both informal and country-style interiors and work very well when combined with curtains. However, they do not provide privacy at a window when the room is illuminated at night.

Contemporary alternatives to pinoleum are woodweave blinds, made from an ever-widening range of woods and grasses from around the world.

Made from environmentally friendly products like bamboo, these blinds can be woven into a variety of patterns to suit any modern home.

Bamboo roll-up blinds are inexpensive and bring an inherent warmth to a room. They can provide an interesting and informal foil for more sumptuous fabrics. The less expensive bamboo roll-up blinds tend to come only in narrow widths, so often more than one will be required on a window.

"Pinoleum blinds allow soft dappled light to filter through"

Pleated blinds

With their strong horizontal lines, pleated blinds are a modern twist on traditional Venetian blinds.

However, they are made with pleated fabric instead of slats which means they cannot be tilted to allow in light.

To filter the light the blinds have to be fully down and to allow light into the room they have to be raised.

When the blind is raised the fabric is folded into 25mm (1in) pleats.

This provides a concertina effect when raised and the pleating is maintained when the blind is lowered.

Upper right A pleated blind offers privacy in this bathroom while still filtering light.

Originally developed for conservatories, they are gaining popularity in other rooms in the house as they are ideal for gently filtering the light without totally darkening the room.

Pleated blinds can be made in a wide range of fabrics from opaque to blackout and can be plain or patterned. They can also be thermally coated to help retain the heat in a room or reflect the sunlight away.

When made to measure these blinds can be cut to fit conservatory ceilings. For vertical windows, pleated blinds can be free-hanging, and for skylights and roof windows aluminium guides can be fitted which hold the blind in position.

Left Pleated blinds fitted in a conservatory reduce glare and heat in the summer and keep in the warmth in winter.

"A modern way to keep the sun and heat at bay"

Roller blinds

These are made from a single flat piece of fabric which is wound round a wooden or metal roller, with a wooden lath at the base.

The fabric rolls off the back of the roller, although you can choose to 'reverse-roll' the fabric and have it roll down in front. This can look more elegant but the blind will stand proud from the window.

The fabric is usually stiffened to keep it flat and to prevent the edges from fraying. For interest, the hem can be shaped and trimmed below the bottom bar.

Although they classically offer excellent sun protection, they are also used as simple window treatments in their own right.

Left Reverse-rolled recess-fitted roller blinds look simple but smart.

The clean and plain lines of roller blinds suit modern interiors where an uncluttered look is the objective. The roller blind can be very attractive on its own or be used in conjunction with other blinds and window treatments.

Roller blinds offer extremes of light management, with the choice of fabrics ranging from sheer to almost total light exclusion.

Translucent roller blinds can offer an attractive alternative to nets and voiles. Blackout roller blinds can aid a good night's sleep in a bedroom, but light will still show around the top and sides. As some roller blind fabrics are moisture-resistant they are immensely practical in kitchens and bathrooms.

They can be operated in two ways. Traditionally blinds were fitted with a spring mechanism and centre pull cord. Nowadays a popular design is the rotary chain mechanism with a cord or bead chain at the side to work the blind. The rotary chain mechanism can be fitted to the left or the right of the blind, depending on your personal preference.

"Roller blinds are ideal when you don't want to lose any light"

Roller blinds can be custom-made, ready-made or you can make them yourself.

There is a wide range of pre-stiffened stock fabrics to choose from when having your blind custom-made. Alternatively, you can have your choice of fabric laminated or stiffened to make it suitable for use as a roller blind.

Having your fabric professionally laminated will mean that you can ensure your blinds match curtains hanging at other windows by using the same fabric, but the blinds can end up being quite thick on the roller. Laminating is a relatively expensive option.

Ready-made roller blinds are an inexpensive choice. They can usually be cut to your window size. The metal roller can be cut with a hacksaw and the fabric can be trimmed with scissors.

Right and far right Bottom-up roller blinds maintain privacy at these unusually shaped windows.

Bottom-up roller blinds are ideal for modern urban living as they pull up from the base to provide privacy, but still allow light to flood in.

Perhaps you have a window that is overlooked at street level or from a distance and you require privacy on the lower half of the window, but still want to let the light in at the top; in this situation this blind is perfect.

This type of blind is fitted at the base of the window and is pulled up, rather than down like a normal roller blind. The cords are fixed to the top of the window with a pulley system and are wound around a cleat.

Bottom-up roller blinds can also be fitted with a cassette box on the window sill which will prevent dust getting into the mechanism.

These blinds are very flexible as they can be drawn all the way up to the top, or halted at any point in between, giving total or selective privacy.

"Choose bottom-up roller blinds for overlooked windows"

Roll-up blinds

A roll-up blind is halfway between a roller blind and a Roman blind.

Offering simple chic, this blind made from soft fabric which rolls up from the bottom. The blind never unwinds completely and keeps a roll of fabric at the base.

This blind is also known as a Swedish blind or a reefed blind.

For low windows or dress blinds it can be rolled up manually and tied in place or it can be operated by cords and pulleys.

Left A roll-up blind works particularly well with curtains.

A roll-up blind is double-sided as the underside is displayed when the blind is rolled up.

This is a wonderful opportunity to use a bold or contrasting fabric on the reverse side for added impact.

But if you choose a fabric that looks good from both sides, then you won't need a second fabric on the reverse.

In Sweden these blinds are traditionally made from gingham which is a double-sided fabric.

As the cords are visible on the front of the blind, decide whether to use a complementing or contrasting coloured cord.

Right Soft and fresh, gingham fabric is teamed perfectly with the face fabric.

"Fabric roll-up blinds are soft and informal"

Roman blinds

Roman blinds are smart and bring tailored elegance to any room.

Roman blinds are flat panels of fabric which are drawn up into a series of deep horizontal folds. To keep the folds looking crisp, the fabric is supported by rods slotted into pockets on the back of the blind. The blind is lowered and lifted by cords threaded through rings attached to the rod pockets. Traditionally the cords are tied off on a cleat.

A popular option for today's windows, their clean-lined look works well in every room in the house and blends in with a variety of furnishings and furniture.

If you are looking to make a statement with strong colours or bold geometric patterns, then Roman blinds work particularly well. However, do bear in mind that the pleating will interrupt strong patterns. Non-geometric patterns can look fussy when made up into Roman blinds and tend to look better when combined with plain curtains. Roman blinds made up in loosely woven linens and cottons will have more of a 'baggy' appearance.

When you have differently sized windows in the same room, curtains everywhere might be overpowering. Choose Roman blinds for the smaller windows and link them to the curtains by making them in the same fabric.

Roman blinds can be bought ready-made, custom-made, or you can make them yourself. Whichever you choose, first decide on whether you want your blind to be unlined, lined or interlined. Then choose the lifting system you want to use.

The least expensive lifting system is the traditional fabric-covered wooden batten with a series of cords, screw eyes and a wall-fixed cleat. For larger and heavier blinds choose a self-locking corded lifting system or a more robust rotary chain mechanism, which will allow you to raise and lower heavier blinds more easily.

There are many techniques used to make Roman blinds. For simplicity we have given instructions for making unlined, lined and interlined blinds, using our standard workroom make-up methods and components. Choose a project to suit your individual sewing skills, as well as your time and patience.

Right A series of Roman blinds are lowered to varying levels, providing light control in a sunny room.

"Roman blinds are a modern alternative to curtains"

An unlined Roman blind is simple to make.

If you use sheer fabrics or light linens these blinds are a
smart alternative to net curtains and are softer than
translucent roller blinds.

Making an unlined Roman blind and machining rod pocket
tape on the reverse is a good project to start on. Once the
blind is made up and the tape is in place, you simply insert
fibreglass rods into the tape and thread cords through the
loops on the tape up to the headrail. If you wish to wash the
blind, the cords and rods can be easily removed.

If you are using a plain fabric and wish to avoid lines of
machine stitching for the rod pocket tape across the blind,
you can seam the fabric to make pockets at the back to
hold the fibreglass rods. Another design variation would be
to seam the pockets on the front of the blind to make a
feature of them.

A key issue when making any Roman blind is to ensure the
folds and rod pockets are square with the bottom of the
blind, otherwise your blind will not draw up evenly.

Lining a Roman blind protects the face fabric from the sun and gives it more weight and body.

Lightweight fabrics, such as cottons, silks and taffetas, will look more sumptuous when lined. In addition the life of your blind will be extended because the lining will reduce the fabric deterioration caused by strong sunlight.

Lining can also carry the rod pockets, which means that the front of your blind will not be defaced by rows of horizontal machine stitching.

For extra body and warmth, Roman blinds can be interlined with a lightweight domett. The interlining is sandwiched between the fabric and the lining.

Roman blinds can also be lined with blackout material but once the laminate has been pierced by a needle during stitching, daylight will come through these small stitch holes. Blackout lining is quite heavy and will increase the overall weight of the finished blind compared to using standard cotton or polycotton lining.

"Lining will extend the life of your Roman blind"

Borders will add extra definition to your Roman blind.

Plain or patterned fabrics are complemented when the sides and lower edge (or lower edge only) are defined with a border.

Borders are also an excellent way to bring contrasting colours and textures into your scheme, while still maintaining simplicity and elegance. Such treatments look better on blinds that are longer than they are wide.

If you wish to have a border on your blind then you need to decide this at the outset as borders have to be attached to the main fabric before the blind is made up.

Borders are usually 2.5 to 10cm (1–4in) in width. You should ensure that the border can be neatly sewn onto the main blind.

"Introduce additional colour and texture with borders and panels"

Insert contrasting panels for a dramatic statement.

The sleek elegance of a Roman blind is complemented by contrasting vertical panels of colour which look particularly striking whether the blind is raised or lowered.

Contrasts have to be bold to work effectively. Use the same fabric but in a different colourway, or combine different textures and colours.

But do make sure the fabric weights are similar, otherwise you might get puckered seams, which would spoil the drama.

If your window is only slightly wider than a single width of fabric, then borders and panels can effectively be used to increase the width of your chosen fabric.

Shaped hems provide additional design detail without extra colours or fabrics.

When choosing a shaped hem, consider the architecture of your window and the design of the fabric you are using. Choose a hem to complement your fabric.

Shaped lower edge blinds are only really suitable for Roman blinds fitted outside the recess. If the blind is fitted into the window recess then the detail at the bottom may let in early morning daylight.

Hems can be made using variations of geometric shapes like triangles and circles, although a combination of curves may work well too.

If you are making your own Roman blind with a shaped hem, make a paper template of your chosen design first. Then place it at the window to see the effect it will have on the room and to check that it will work with your chosen blind fabric. Adjust the shaping if necessary. When you start making your blind, you will shape the hem section before you start making the main part.

Left The zigzag hem on this Roman blind is matched to the width of the stripes. The points are finished with bobbles.

Add trimming for an individual finish to
your blind.

The choice of trimmings and edgings are infinite; fringing,
braid, ribbon, beads, crystals or lace are some of the
possibilities. Trimmings can be bold and daring or restrained
and subtle.

Delicate beads and crystals will work better on blinds that
hang outside the recess as they may be damaged by the
window sill when the blind is let down.

Fringes or beads can be hand-sewn onto the lower edge of
the blind once the blind has been made.

An edging can personalise a ready-made blind and help it
blend into your room design. You may want to repeat fringes
or trimmings already used in the room.

"Flat braids sewn onto Roman blinds can look striking"

Blind essentials and make-up

This section covers the practical issues surrounding blinds: measuring, estimating fabric and making roller, roll-up and Roman blinds. Step-by-step instructions will show you how to make unlined, lined, and interlined Roman blinds on wooden battens, corded or rotary chain aluminium headrails.

MEASURING FOR BLINDS

It is well worth allowing yourself time to measure accurately; don't rush it. Measure with a steel tape measure rather than a fabric one as the latter type can stretch over time. Take your measurements in either metric or Imperial – don't mix the two. If you decide to measure in metric then use one standard, either millimetres or centimetres. Finally, the best advice we can give you is to always double-check your measurements and make a careful note of them.

Begin by deciding on whether you want your blind to fit inside or outside the recess.

If you fit a blind inside the recess then you will lose some light as the blind will stack up into the top of the window when pulled up. Check that the blind can be fitted into the recess and will not interfere with the window opening or catches.

If you fit outside the recess then you lose less light when the blind is drawn up. This can make a window appear larger and leaves the window sill free for ornaments.

Draw yourself a diagram of the window and note all your measurements. Never assume that two apparently identical windows are exactly the same – measure each window individually. For hard blinds, follow the manufacturer's specific measuring instructions.

You will also need to decide on whether you want to operate the blind from the left or right.

Do consider cord and chain safety and be aware of the hazard that can be posed by unrestrained cords and chains. In children's rooms cords and chains can be looped through safety clips and held back against the wall.

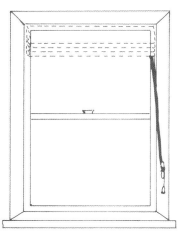

Blind fitted inside recess

Blind fitted outside recess

MEASURING INSIDE A RECESS

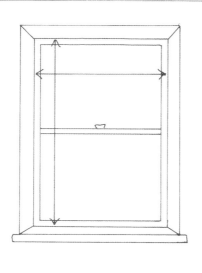

Measure the width of the recess in three places and note the shortest measurement. Repeat for the drop.

ESTABLISHING THE FINISHED WIDTH OF YOUR RECESS-FIXED BLIND

When making up your blind you should always work to the smallest point; this will be your finished blind width.

ESTABLISHING THE FINISHED LENGTH OF YOUR RECESS-FIXED BLIND

To establish the finished length of a recess-fixed blind, measure from the top of the recess to the window sill. This will be your finished length.

Professional tip

*Blinds fitted outside the recess are usually fitted
5 to 30cm (2–12in) above the window.
They can be fitted to the face of the window architrave, or
above it. This is known as face-fixing.*

MEASURING OUTSIDE A RECESS

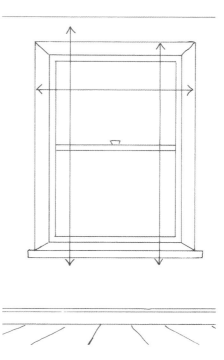

Take three measurements across the window including the frame/architrave and note the largest. Measure the drop from the top of the window, or above the window.

ESTABLISHING THE FINISHED WIDTH OF YOUR FACE-FIXED BLIND

There are two ways to establish the finished width of your blind. If your window has an architrave, then measure across the window and include the architraves at each side. You can then make your blind to this width. Alternatively, you can measure the width of the window sill and make your blind to this width. If your window has no architrave or sill then extend the blind 5 to 10cm (2–4in) either side.

ESTABLISHING THE FINISHED LENGTH OF YOUR FACE-FIXED BLIND

Fit the wooden batten or headrail in position and measure down to just below the sill. This will be your finished length. If your window sill projects further out into the room than the batten or headrail, then the blind can be made to finish at the top of the sill.

CALCULATING CUT WIDTHS AND CUT DROPS FOR SOFT BLINDS

Having measured your window and established the finished width and finished length of your blind, you now need to calculate the cut width and cut drop of your blind so that you can estimate how much fabric you need to buy. Cut widths and cut drops are the finished width and length of your blind plus side turning and hem allowances.

ROLLER BLINDS

To calculate the cut width add 5 to 10cm (2–4in) to the finished width of your blind to allow for shrinkage when the fabric is treated with a stiffening spray.

To calculate the cut drop add 30cm (12in) to the finished length to allow for a 5cm (2in) hem allowance; the remaining fabric will be wound onto the roller. You also need to add a stiffening and shrinkage allowance of 5 to 10cm (2–4in) to the length.

ROLL-UP BLINDS

Calculate as for a Roman blind below but add an extra 40cm (16in) to the length for the batten, the bottom dowel and the permanently rolled bottom section. Remember that the blind is double-sided so you will need fabric for both the front and the back.

ROMAN BLINDS

To calculate the cut width of your blind, add 16cm (6in) side turning allowance to the finished width for an unlined blind and 8cm (3in) for lined and interlined blinds.

To calculate the cut drop, take the finished blind length and add 6cm (2¼in) for heading and hem allowances. If making a blind with a wooden batten headrail add an extra 30cm (12in). This additional fabric allows extra to cover the batten.

If making a lined or interlined blind, purchase the same amount of lining or interlining as your main blind fabric.

ESTIMATING FABRIC QUANTITES FOR PLAIN FABRICS

Now you have your cut width, divide this figure by the width of your fabric. Round up this figure to the nearest width to work out how many fabric widths you will need to buy.

EXAMPLE

Cut width = 160cm

160cm ÷ 137cm wide fabric = 1.167
Round this figure up to two widths

Cut drop = 200cm

2 widths x 200cm cut drop = 400cm of fabric required.

Professional tip

To quickly calculate how many widths of fabric you will need to buy, use the table below.

FINISHED WIDTH OF BLIND	NUMBER OF WIDTHS REQUIRED (using 137cm (54in) wide fabric)
Up to 128cm (50in)	1
129–260cm (51–102in)	2
261–300cm (103–118in)	3

ESTIMATING FABRIC QUANTITIES FOR PATTERNED FABRICS

For patterned fabric ask the fabric shop for the pattern repeat. Divide the cut drop by the pattern repeat and round up to the nearest whole number – never round down. Multiply the result by the pattern repeat. This will give you your adjusted cut drop.

Now multiply your adjusted cut drop by the number of widths of fabric required and add one extra repeat so you can choose exactly where on the pattern repeat the top of your blind will start.

EXAMPLE

Cut drop = 200cm
Pattern repeat = 18cm

200cm ÷ 18cm = 11.11
Round this up to 12

12 x 18cm = 216cm adjusted cut drop

(2 widths x 216cm) + 18cm = 450cm of fabric required.

NOTE ABOUT FABRIC WIDTHS

Most fabrics, linings and interlinings come in widths of 137cm (54in). However, some silks come in widths of 120cm (48in) and some cottons come in widths of 150cm (60in). Also modern machinery can produce some fabrics in wider widths of 280cm (110in) and 300cm (118in).

If your Roman or roll-up blind is only slightly wider than the width of the fabric you can use one of these options:

1   If the blind is wide, but the cut length is just less than the maximum width of the fabric, the fabric can be turned on its side and used lengthways. This really only applies if your fabric is plain, or has a pattern that will work horizontally as well as vertically. This will eliminate the need to sew widths of fabric together. If required, you can turn lining and interlining sideways as well.

2   If your blind width is only slightly wider than the fabric, you can add a border (as below) or insert a panel using a contrasting fabric. See bordered blinds on pages 66–7 for instructions on how to do this.

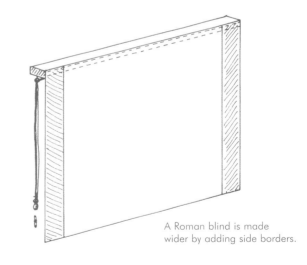

A Roman blind is made wider by adding side borders.

SEAMING WIDTHS OF FABRIC TOGETHER

If you need two widths of fabric for your blind, cut one width into two and seam to the centre panel at each side. Always have a full-width centre panel in the middle of the blind. For details on seaming see page 94.

Making roller blinds

Making a roller blind using a kit requires little sewing. Kits contain everything you need except the fabric and fabric stiffener. Use tightly woven fabrics. Homemade roller blinds suit small and medium windows.

Your roller blind kit will contain: a roller with a self-adhesive strip, universal brackets, bottom bar, and control mechanism including fittings.

CHOOSING A FABRIC

For roller blinds it is best to avoid seams in the fabric as the bulk of the seam could wind round the roller unevenly.

If you intend to stiffen the fabric with a stiffening solution, choose a fabric with a relatively close weave that will not fray. Avoid heavyweight or loosely woven fabrics. If you find that the stiffened cut edges do fray, especially if the sides catch the side winder, use an anti-fray spray to prevent this.

If you don't stiffen the fabric, it is possible to neaten the edges by sewing side turnings. This option is suitable for fine fabrics and for blinds with a relatively short drop. However, be aware that the extra thickness of fabric created by the side turnings will cause ruckles in the centre of the blind which you may find unattractive.

STIFFENING THE FABRIC

To stiffen the fabric follow the manufacturer's instructions. However, it is sensible to test a small sample of the fabric first.

Cut the fabric larger than the size needed to allow for shrinkage. Iron out any creases before you apply the solution.

To support the fabric and to hold it taut, staple the top and bottom edges onto two pieces of wood, taking care to keep the grain of the fabric straight.

Hang the wood over a door or suitable structure in a well ventilated area and spray the back of the fabric with the solution. A second application will help limp fabrics.

MAKING A ROLLER BLIND ·

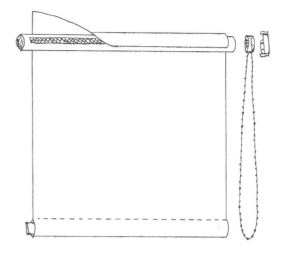

1   Read the roller blind kit instructions carefully.

2   To get the exact width of your roller blind, fit the brackets in position.

3   Cut the roller to fit between the brackets.

4   Stiffen the fabric if necessary, and allow to dry.

5   Cut the fabric to the width of the roller minus 1cm (⅜in) and add 20cm (8in) to the length to allow for the heading and bottom bar. You can use a set square to make sure the corners are exact right angles.

6   Use anti-fray spray on the edges of loosely woven fabrics.

7   To make the pocket for the bottom bar, turn up a hem that is at least 3cm (1¼in) deep, and stitch, closing one end.

8   Trim the bottom bar so that it is 1cm (⅜in) shorter than the blind, insert it and slip-stitch the open end closed.

9   Place the roller at the head of the fabric and remove the self-adhesive strip. Carefully place the fabric and the roller together ensuring that the fabric is perfectly straight and square to the roller tube.

10 Roll the blind tightly and slot it into the brackets.

Professional tip

If the blind will not roll up evenly check the following points:

Are the brackets level?

Has the top edge of the fabric been fixed onto the roller absolutely level?

Have the sides of the fabric been cut parallel?

YOU WILL NEED

Roller blind kit
Fabric
Junior hacksaw
Fabric stiffener
Set square

Making roll-up blinds

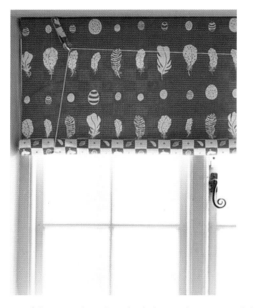

In a variation of the procedure described, the cords are carried through rings on loops of fabric instead of the front screw eyes.

1   Before starting on your blind, first establish the finished width and length. See page 41 for how to do this.

2   Cut the two fabrics to the finished measurements of the blind adding 4cm (1½in) to the width and 40cm (16in) to the length.

3   Place right sides of the two fabrics together and mark with pins the 2cm (¾in) side and hem turning allowances.

4   Stitch down the sides and along the bottom. Remove the pins, clip the corners, then turn right sides out and press.

5   Cut the dowel to the width of the finished blind minus 1cm (⅜in) and place the dowel inside the bottom of the blind. Machine as close as possible to the dowel with a zip foot to enclose it into the hem.

6   To hold the two fabrics together sew small 'spot tack' stitches through the fabrics 10cm (4in) in from each end at regular intervals up the fabric (see page 134). If your blind is wider than 60cm (24in) you will need to sew additional 'spot tacks' spaced equally no more than 35cm (14in) apart across the blind. If you match the colour of your thread to your fabric the stitching will be barely visible from the right side of the blind.

7   Working on the right side of the blind, measure up from the bottom of the hem to the finished length of the blind and mark the top with a row of pins. At the pin line fold over the remaining fabric to the back. Cut off the excess fabric to 1.5cm (⅝in). Cut the loop Velcro to the finished width of the blind. With the wrong side uppermost pin the Velcro to the top of the blind. Now machine the top, bottom and sides of the Velcro ensuring you have concealed the raw edges of the fabrics.

8   With a small wood saw, cut the wooden batten to the same width as the finished blind less 1cm (⅜in). Fold the fabric round the batten and staple in place, making sure the raw edges are hidden at the back of the batten.

9   Staple the hook side of the Velcro onto the top edge of the batten.

10 Using the bradawl to start the holes, fix two of the screw eyes to the underside of the batten, placing them side on, 15 to 30cm (6–12in) in from each end, depending on the width of the blind. This is where the cords will go.

11 Using the bradawl, prepare the holes for the screw eyes in the front of the batten, positioning two of them in line with the eyes below and the final one very close to the right-hand side for right-hand-side operation.

Steps 10–11

12 Velcro the blind to the top edge of the batten. Insert two screw eyes into the front edge of the batten through the fabric, aligning them with the ones at the back. Insert the remaining screw eye into the batten on the right-hand side.

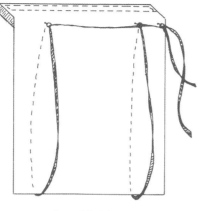

Steps 12–14

13 Cut two lengths of cord: one three times the length of the blind, and one three times the length of the blind plus once the width.

14 Tie the longer cord to the back screw eye on the left-hand side and the other cord to the back screw eye on the right-hand side. Starting with the longer cord, bring it down the back of the blind, up the front and thread through each of the screw eyes at the front of the blind. Follow the same procedure for the second cord but just thread through the two screw eyes at the front.

15 Tension the cords by pulling them taut and attach a wooden acorn. Pull to roll up the blind.

16 Screw brackets onto underside of the batten and fit at the window.

Professional tip

If your window is wide, add more screw eyes or ties spaced equally 35cm (14in) apart across the blind. Support the centre of the batten with an extra angle bracket.

ROLL-UP BLIND WITH TIES

Follow steps **1–6**, then:

1 Make four ties 5cm (2in) wide by twice the length of the blind plus 10cm (4in). See page 131, steps **5–6**, for instructions on making ties.

2 Attach two ties to the back of the blind and two ties to the front of the blind, placing them 15 to 30cm (6–12in) in from the edges.

3 Make up the blind as before, omitting steps **10** and **11**. Velcro the blind to the top edge of the batten, then roll up the blind and tie bows to secure in place.

Step 16

YOU WILL NEED

Face fabric
Reverse fabric
5cm x 2.5cm
(2in x 1in) wooden batten, the width of the blind
1cm (⅜in) dowel or slim pole
5 (or more) screw eyes and blind cord,
or extra fabric for ties
Velcro
Bradawl
Staple gun and 8mm staples
Wooden acorn
Cleat
2 angle brackets, 3.5cm x 3.5cm (1½in x 1½in)
Set square
1.5m metal ruler
Sewing kit
Tool kit for fitting

Making Roman blinds

By now you will have measured your windows, established your finished width and length of your Roman blind and estimated your fabric quantities. The following pages will provide you with everything else you need to know to make your Roman blind.

Before you start working on your fabric, take the time to read these instructions carefully. The next thing you will have to do is work out your folds, either standard or cascaded. Then you choose the type of blind – unlined, lined or interlined – before fitting it to your chosen headrail – wooden batten, corded track or rotary chain.

ROMAN BLIND STANDARD FOLD TABLE

Working out the most appropriate fold sizes and numbers of rod pockets for Roman blinds can seem daunting. However, if you want your blind to fit outside the recess, then you can use the table opposite to easily and quickly work out the number of folds and rod pockets you will need.

1 Decide on the headrail you want to use. See page 62 for descriptions of the three types available.

2 Establish the approximate finished length of your blinds (see page 41).

3 Deduct the appropriate headrail allowance from your finished blind length to establish the amount of fabric to be folded.

4 Taking the length of fabric to be folded, find the closest measurement to this on the table.

EXAMPLE

If your blind is approximately 105cm in length and you have chosen a rotary chain headrail, deduct the 10cm headrail allowance from the finished blind length.

This leaves 95cm of fabric to be folded. Now you could select one of the following folded fabric lengths: 100cm length with five 20cm folds and two rod pockets, or 105cm length with seven 15cm folds and three rod pockets.

If you choose a smaller fold size then the depth of the blind when pulled up will be reduced.

Add the 10cm headrail allowance to the chosen fabric length to be folded to get your finished blind length. Now follow the make-up instructions for your preferred Roman blind.

ROMAN BLIND STANDARD FOLD TABLE

Finished blind length = fabric to be folded + headrail allowance

Headrail allowance
Wooden batten, 5cm (2in)
Corded headrail, 6–7.5cm (2¼–3in)
Rotary chain headrail, 10cm (4in)

Fabric to be folded	Optional fold depth	No. of pleat sections
45cm (18in) 60cm (24in)	15cm (6in) 20cm (8in)	3 sections (1 rod pocket)
75cm (30in) 100cm (40in)	15cm (6in) 20cm (8in)	5 sections (2 rod pockets)
105cm (42in) 140cm (56in)	15cm (6in) 20cm (8in)	7 sections (3 rod pockets)
135cm (54in) 180cm (72in)	15cm (6in) 20cm (8in)	9 sections (4 rod pockets)
165cm (66in) 220cm (88in)	15cm (6in) 20cm (8in)	11 sections (5 rod pockets)
195cm (78in) 260cm (104in)	15cm (6in) 20cm (8in)	13 sections (6 rod pockets)
225cm (90in) 300cm (120in)	15cm (6in) 20cm (8in)	15 sections (7 rod pockets)
255cm (102in) 340cm (136in)	15cm (6in) 20cm (8in)	17 sections (8 rod pockets)

HEADRAIL ALLOWANCE

This is the measurement from the top of the blind to the bottom of the lifting mechanism, i.e. screw eyes, cord lock or the rotary chain mechanism.

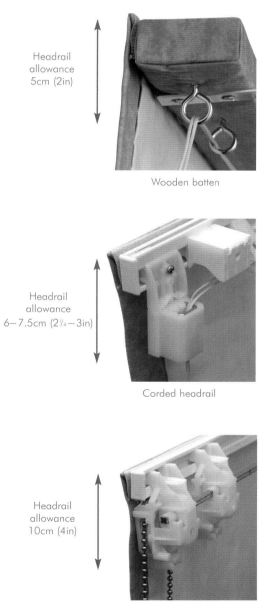

Headrail allowance 5cm (2in)

Wooden batten

Headrail allowance 6–7.5cm (2¼–3in)

Corded headrail

Headrail allowance 10cm (4in)

Rotary chain headrail

ROMAN BLIND STANDARD FOLD CALCULATIONS

If you are fitting your Roman blind inside the recess or you prefer to do your own fold calculations, then follow these instructions to establish the number of folds and rod pockets for your blind. Standard pleating is where the folds lie on top of each other when the blind is drawn up. You will need a calculator for this part!

1 Establish the finished length of the Roman blind (see page 41).

2 Deduct your headrail allowance from the finished length of the blind to establish the fabric to be folded (see page 49 for headrail allowances).

3 Decide on the approximate depth of the folds you would like on your blind when it is drawn up. Folds are usually between 10 and 25cm (4–10in) in depth, depending on how tightly you want your blind to stack up.

4 Now divide the length of the fabric to be folded by an odd number until you reach an answer closest to your desired fold depth. The odd number you divide by will give you the number of pleat sections for your blind.

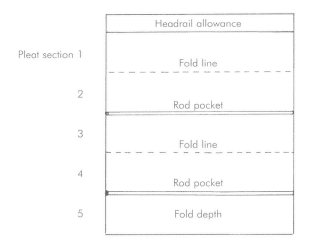

EXAMPLE

The finished blind length is 100cm and will be fitted on a rotary chain headrail. You have decided you would like approximately 16cm-deep folds.

First deduct 10cm headrail allowance from the finished length of your blind = 90cm.

Now divide this figure by 3, 5, 7 and 9

$$90cm \div 3 = 30cm$$
$$90cm \div 5 = 18cm$$
$$90cm \div 7 = 12.86cm$$
$$90cm \div 9 = 10cm$$

You can see that dividing by 5 gives you an answer closest to your desired fold depth of 16cm, so your blind will have 5 pleat sections, each of 18cm. Looking at the Roman blind standard fold table on page 49, you can also see that the 5-pleat arrangement has 2 rod pockets.

Starting at the bottom of your blind, you will have a rod pocket 18cm up, then a fold another 18cm up, and so on until you have your 5 sections. Then add your 10cm headrail allowance.

It is helpful if you draw a diagram showing the pleat sections with rod pockets, folds and measurements. You can also make a folded paper version of your blind to make sure you are happy with the folds and your calculations.

Standard fold pleated-up blind

ROMAN BLIND CASCADE FOLD CALCULATIONS

Cascade pleating is where the folds are staggered or stepped, creating a cascade effect when the blind is drawn up.

Follow steps 1–3 as for standard fold calculations. Then:

1   Decide on the cascade amount, usually between 1cm (⅜in) and 5cm (2in). This will be the difference in measurement between the pleat sections.

2   Add the cascade amount for each pleat section together to arrive at a total amount. Working from the top of the blind, allow 0cm for pleat sections 1 and 2. Sections 3 and 4 are the predetermined 3cm cascade and each pair of sections after that will have another 3cm added.

    If your blind has 5 pleat sections the calculations are:

Section	1	2	3	4	5	Total Cascade
Cascade Allowance	+0cm	+0cm	+3cm	+3cm	+6cm	=12cm

3   Deduct the total cascade amount from the length of your blind (minus the headrail allowance). Divide this figure by the number of pleat sections. Now add the cascade allowances back onto each section to determine the cascaded pleat sizes.

EXAMPLE

The finished blind length is 92cm and will be fitted on a rotary chain headrail. You have decided on 5 pleat sections with a 3cm cascade.

First deduct 10cm headrail allowance from the length of your blind = 82cm

Calculate the total cascade allowance
= 0cm + 0cm + 3cm + 3cm + 6cm = 12cm

Deduct the total cascade allowance
82cm minus 12cm = 70cm

Divide this figure by the pleat sections
70cm ÷ 5 = 14cm

Now add the cascade allowance back onto each section.

Pleat section	Pleat size without cascade	Cascade allowance	Cascaded pleat size
1	14cm	+0cm	=14cm
2	14cm	+0cm	=14cm
3	14cm	+3cm	=17cm
4	14cm	+3cm	=17cm
5	14cm	+6cm	=20cm

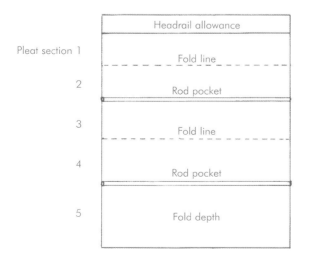

Cascade fold pleated-up blind

CASCADE PLEATING WITH A BOTTOM FLAP

This is a variation on a cascaded Roman blind. Instead of the blind pleating up evenly into cascaded folds, the bottom fold is longer, leaving a decorative flap at the bottom of the blind. Calculating the fold sections is more involved than the standard or cascade method, so do follow the instructions carefully and draw a diagram to double-check your figures.

1   Establish the finished length of the blind.

2   Decide on the depth of your flap. Flaps can range from 2 to 20cm ($\frac{3}{4}$–8in), depending on the effect you want.

3   Deduct your flap depth and headrail allowance from the finished length to leave the amount of fabric to be folded.

4   Decide on the approximate depth of the folds you would like on your blind when it is drawn up.

5   Now divide the length of the fabric to be folded by an odd number until you reach an answer closest to your desired fold depth. The odd number you divide by will give you the number of pleat sections for your blind.

6   Decide on the cascade amount, usually between 1 and 5cm ($\frac{3}{8}$–2in). This will be the difference in measurement between the pleat sections.

7   Add the cascade amount for each pleat section together to arrive at a total amount. Note that the bottom three pleat sections must have the same cascade allowance added back.

8   Deduct the total cascade amount from the fabric to be folded. Divide this adjusted figure by the number of pleat sections.

9   Now add the cascade allowances back onto each section to determine the cascaded rod pocket and fold sizes. Working from the top of the blind, allow 0cm for pleat sections 1 and 2. Sections 3 and 4 are the predetermined cascade amount and each pair of sections after that will be increased in size by the cascade amount. Remember that the last three pleat sections must have the same cascade allowance added back.

10 Add the flap depth to the lowest section.

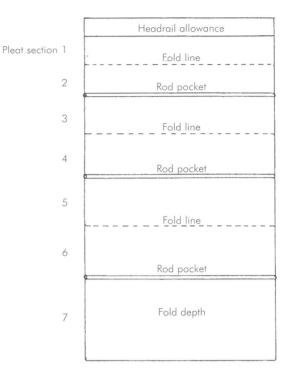

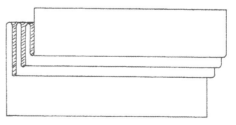

Cascade fold pleated-up blind with a bottom flap

EXAMPLE

The finished blind length is 121cm. Deduct flap depth of 10cm and headrail allowance of 10cm. Fabric to be folded is now 101cm.

Folds are to be approximately 15cm. Dividing 101cm by 7 obtains the closest figure to 15cm. This means the blind will have 7 sections and 3 rod pockets.

Cascade allowance is to be 3cm. Add up the total allowances for each section. Remember that the last three sections must have the same cascade allowance.

Section	1	2	3	4	5	6	7	Total cascade
Cascade Allowance	+0cm	+0cm	+0cm	+3cm	+6cm	+6cm	+6cm	=24cm

Deduct cascade allowance from the fabric length 101cm minus 24cm = 77cm

Now divide this figure by the number of sections 77cm ÷ 7 = 11

Now add the cascade allowances back onto each section.

Pleat section	Pleat size without cascade	Cascade allowance	Cascaded pleat size
1	11cm	+0cm	=11cm
2	11cm	+0cm	=11cm
3	11cm	+3cm	=14cm
4	11cm	+3cm	=14cm
5	11cm	+6cm	=17cm
6	11cm	+6cm	=17cm
7	11cm	+6cm	=17cm

Add the flap depth to the lowest section.

To double-check your calculations, add up all of the cascaded pleats, plus the flap depth and headrail allowance. You should arrive back at the finished blind length.

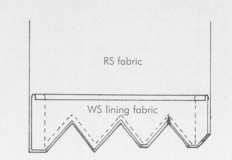
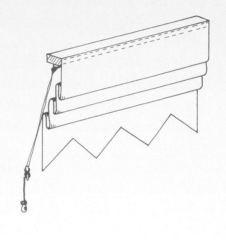

Making unlined Roman blinds

Finished unlined Roman blind, ready to be corded and attached to the headrail.

1 Before starting on your blind, first establish the finished size. See page 41 for how to do this.

2 Decide on the headrail for your blind. See page 62 for details.

3 Calculate your rod tape pocket spacing and number of folds. Use one of the methods on pages 48–53.

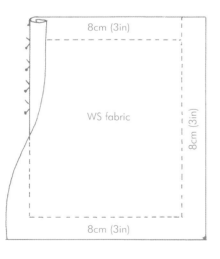

Steps 4–6

4 Cut the fabric to the finished measurements of the blind, adding 8cm (3in) to each side, 8cm (3in) to the top and 8cm (3in) to the bottom for turning allowances.

5 On the right side of the fabric mark with pins the 8cm (3in) side turning allowances.

6 Lay the fabric onto the table with the wrong side uppermost. Using the pin lines as a guide, fold in 4cm (1½in) twice down the sides, pin in place and hand-sew or machine. Remove the pins.

7 Fold in 4cm (1½in) twice on the lower edge, pin in place and hand-sew or machine across. Remove the pins. Leave the hem open at one side to insert the aluminium bottom bar later.

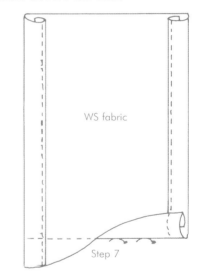

Step 7

8 Measuring up from the bottom of the blind, at each side edge of the fabric mark the position of the first rod pocket with a fabric marker. Lay your metal ruler across both marks and use a set square to ensure that the line is square with the side edges of the blind. Now draw a line horizontally across the fabric.

9 Cut the rod pocket tape to the width of the blind. To neaten the cut edges of the tape turn them in 1cm (⅜in) twice. With the open slits facing the top of the blind pin the rod pocket tape onto the marked line, setting it in 2cm (¾in) from the side edges, and machine in place. Working up from the seam, repeat the measuring, marking, pinning and machining for all the other rod pocket tape positions.

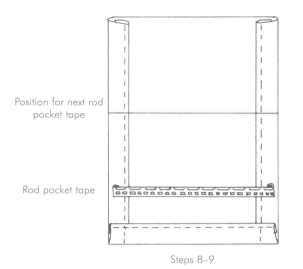

Position for next rod pocket tape

Rod pocket tape

Steps 8–9

10 Working on the right side of the blind, measure up from the bottom of the hem to the finished length of the blind and mark the top with a row of pins. At the pin line fold over the remaining fabric to the back. Cut off the excess fabric to 1.5cm (⅝in). Cut the loop Velcro to the finished width of the blind. With wrong side uppermost pin the Velcro to the top of the blind. Now machine the top, bottom and sides of the Velcro, ensuring you have concealed the raw edges of the fabric.

11 Cut the required number of fibreglass rods to the width of the rod pocket tape minus 1cm (⅜in). Take care at this point as fibreglass splinters, so make sure you wear protective gloves and wrap masking tape around the cutting area before cutting the rods with a hacksaw. Fit the plastic end caps at each end of the rods. Now slide the rods into the rod pocket tape through the slits at the top.

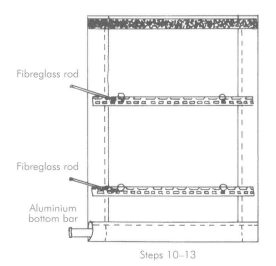

Fibreglass rod

Fibreglass rod

Aluminium bottom bar

Steps 10–13

12 With a junior hacksaw, cut the aluminium bottom bar to the width of the blind less 2cm (¾in). Brush away any metal dust and fit the plastic end caps. Slide the bar through the opening at the hem of the blind and close the opening with slip stitches (see page 134).

13 Sew the rings to the rod pocket tape 10cm (4in) in from each side. If your blind is wider than 60cm (24in) you will need to attach additional rings equally spaced approximately 35cm (14in) apart across the blind.

14 To complete your blind, follow the fitting instructions for your chosen headrail from pages 63–5.

YOU WILL NEED

Fabric
Lining
Roman blind kit or separate
components listed below:
Headrail (see page 62)
Fibreglass rods and end caps
2.5cm (1in) aluminium bottom
bar and end caps
12mm (½in) plastic or brass
rings, 2 or more per rod
2cm (¾in) hook and loop
Velcro
Large set square
1.5m metal ruler
Sewing kit
Fabric marker
Junior hacksaw

Making lined Roman blinds

LINED ROMAN BLIND WITH LINING ROD POCKETS

The rod pockets are formed from the lining.

1 Before starting on your blind, first establish the finished size. See page 41 for how to do this.

2 Decide on the headrail. See page 62 for details.

3 Calculate your rod pocket spacing and number of folds. Use one of the methods on pages 48–53.

4 Cut the fabric to the finished measurements of the blind adding 4cm (1½in) to each side, to the top and to the bottom for turning allowances.

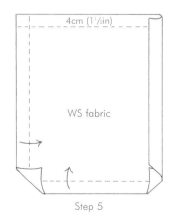

4cm (1½in)

WS fabric

Step 5

5 On the right side of the fabric mark the 4cm (1½in) side and 4cm (1½in) bottom turning allowances with pins. The intersection of the side and bottom lines will be the corners of your blind. With the right side of the fabric uppermost, pierce through the two corner mitre points with pins. The corner pins will help you fold the corners accurately.

WS fabric

Step 6

6 Working on the wrong side of the fabric, turn each lower hem corner up 45° so that the corner pin is in the middle of the fold. Turn the side edges up 4cm (1½in) along the pin line and pin in place. To complete the mitred corners fold up the lower edge 4cm (1½in) along the pin line and pin in place. Now remove the pins used to mark the turnings

7 Cut out the lining to the finished width of the blind and the length of the blind plus an extra 2cm (¾in) per rod pocket and for unforeseen circumstances add an extra 5cm (2in) to the length.

8 On the wrong side of the lining fold and press in 2cm (¾in) down each side.

9 With the right side of the lining facing you, measure up from the bottom and at each side edge of the fabric mark the position of the first rod pocket with a fabric marker. Lay your metal ruler across both marks and use a set square to ensure that the line is square with the side edge. Now draw a line horizontally across the fabric. Measure up 2cm (¾in) from this line and draw another horizontal line across the lining, again ensuring it is square with the side edge.

10 Fold the wrong sides together to align the horizontal lines, and machine them to form a rod pocket. Working up from your rod pocket seam, repeat the measuring, marking and sewing steps until you have

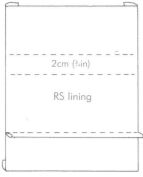

Steps 9–10

made the required number of rod pockets. Although this may seem tedious, only by marking and sewing one pocket at a time will you compensate for any small discrepancies in the widths of your rod pocket sizes.

11 Turn up the hem of the lining 2cm (³/₄in). Pin the lining onto the back of the blind 2cm (³/₄in) in from the sides and 2cm (³/₄in) up from the hem. Before you start sewing the lining in position, double-check that the first rod pocket is in the correct position. If necessary adjust the position of the lining. Slip-stitch down each side and along the hem, taking care not to stitch through to the front of the blind.

12 To hold the fabric and lining together sew small 'spot tack' stitches through the two fabrics just on the fabric pocket machine lines, 10cm (4in) in from each end. If your blind is wider than 60cm (24in) you will need to sew additional 'spot tacks' spaced equally no more than 35cm (14in) apart across the blind (see page 134). If you match the colour of your thread to your fabric the stitching will be barely visible from the right side of the blind.

13 Working on the right side of the blind, measure up from the bottom of the hem to the finished length of the blind and mark the top with a row of pins. At the pin line fold over the remaining fabric to the back. Cut off the excess fabric to 1.5cm (⁵/₈in). Cut the loop Velcro to the finished width of the blind. With wrong side uppermost pin the Velcro to the top of the blind. Now machine the top, bottom and sides of the Velcro, ensuring you have concealed the raw edges of the fabric.

14 Cut the required number of fibreglass rods to the width of the rod pockets minus 1cm (³/₈in). Take care at this point as fibreglass splinters, so make sure you wear protective gloves and wrap masking tape

around the cutting area before cutting the rods with a hacksaw. Fit the plastic end caps at each end of the rods. Now slide the rods into the rod pockets and and hand-sew the side openings closed.

15 With a junior hacksaw, cut the aluminium bottom bar to the width of the blind less 2cm (³/₄in). Brush away any metal dust and fit the plastic end caps at the end of the bar. Slide the bar through the opening left at the hem of the blind and close the opening with slip stitches (see page 134).

16 Sew the rings to the rod pockets 10cm (4in) in from each side. If your blind is wider than 60cm (24in) you will need to attach additional rings spaced equally no more than 35cm (14in) apart across the blind.

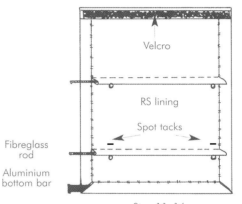

Velcro

RS lining

Spot tacks

Fibreglass rod

Aluminium bottom bar

Step 11–16

17 To complete your blind, follow the fitting instructions for your chosen headrail from pages 62–5.

YOU WILL NEED

Fabric

Lining

Roman blind kit or separate components listed below:

Headrail (see page 62)

Fibreglass rods and end caps

2.5cm (1in) aluminium bottom bar and end caps

12mm (½in) plastic or brass rings, 2 or more per rod

20mm (⅞in) hook and loop Velcro

Large set square

1.5m metal ruler

Sewing kit

Fabric marker

Junior hacksaw

Making interlined Roman blinds

Attaching the lining to an interlined Roman blind.

An interlined blind has a soft extra layer 'sandwiched' between the fabric and lining, which makes the blind look more sumptuous.

Interlining a Roman blind is an advanced make-up technique and is not recommended as your first sewing project. It involves more sewing than making unlined and lined blinds.

Choose a lightweight interlining such as domett (160g/m²) or a sarril (140g/m²). Interlining will increase the weight of the finished blind so it will be heavier to pull up.

To prevent the blind sagging due to the extra weight of the interlining, we place a 1cm (³⁄₈in) diameter weighted pole in the lowest rod pocket.

Follow steps **1–5** given for the lined Roman blind.

1 Cut the interlining to the same size as the blind fabric.

2 With the wrong side uppermost place your interlining on top of the blind fabric. Secure the interlining with horizontal rows of interlocking stitches (see page 134) at each rod pocket and fold line.

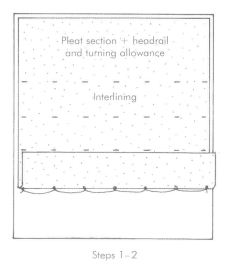

Steps 1–2

3 Turn each lower hem corner up 45° so that the corner pin is in the middle of the fold. Turn the lower edge up 4cm (1¹⁄₂in) along the pin line and pin in place. To complete the mitred corners fold in the sides by 4cm (1¹⁄₂in) along the pin line and pin in place. Remove the pins.

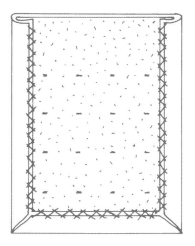

Steps 3–4

4   Herringbone-stitch (see page 134) along the sides
    and bottom turning, leaving one mitred corner open
    to insert your aluminium bottom bar later.

5   Cut out the lining to the finished width of the blind
    and the length of the blind plus an extra 2cm (³/₄in)
    per rod pocket, and for unforeseen circumstances,
    add an extra 5cm (2in) to the length.

6   On the wrong side of the lining fold and press in
    2cm (³/₄in) down each side.

7   With the right side of the lining uppermost, measure
    up from the bottom and at each side edge of the
    fabric mark the position of the first rod pocket with a
    fabric marker. Lay your metal ruler across both marks
    and use a set square to ensure that the line is square
    with the side edge. Now draw a line horizontally
    across the fabric. Measure up 4cm (1¹/₂cm) from
    this line and draw another horizontal line across the
    lining, again ensuring it is square with the side edge.
    This pocket will hold your 1cm (³/₈in) white plastic-
    coated weighted rod, so the first pocket will be larger
    than the rest.

8   Fold the wrong sides together to align the horizontal
    lines, and machine along the lines to form the rod
    pocket.

9   Measure up from the first seam and mark the
    position of the next rod pocket at each edge of the
    fabric. Lay your metal ruler across both marks and
    use a set square to ensure that the line is square with
    the side edges. Now draw a line horizontally across
    the fabric. Measure up 2cm (³/₄in) from this line and
    draw another horizontal line across the lining, again
    ensuring it is square with the side edge.

10 As for the first pocket, fold the wrong sides together
    to align the horizontal lines, and machine along the
    lines to form a rod pocket.

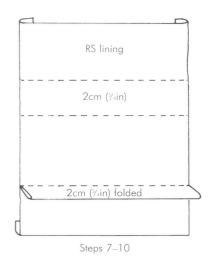

Steps 7–10

11 Repeat steps **7–10**, measuring, marking and sewing,
    until you have made the required number of rod
    pockets. Although this may seem tedious, only by
    marking and sewing one pocket at a time will you
    compensate for any small discrepancies in the widths
    of your rod pocket sizes.

YOU WILL NEED

Fabric
Lining
Interlining (domett 160g/m² or
sarill 140g/m²)
Headrail (see page 62)
1cm (³/₈in) diameter white
plastic-coated weighted rod
and end caps
Fibreglass rods and end caps
2.5cm (1in) aluminium bottom
bar and end caps
12mm (¹/₂in) plastic or brass
rings, 2 or more per rod
2cm (³/₄in) loop Velcro
Set square
1.5m metal ruler
Sewing kit
Fabric marker
Junior hacksaw

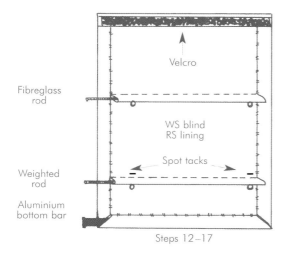

Velcro

Fibreglass
rod

WS blind
RS lining

Spot tacks

Weighted
rod

Aluminium
bottom bar

Steps 12–17

12 Turn up the hem of the lining 2cm (³⁄₄in). Pin the bottom edge of the lining onto the back of the blind 2cm (³⁄₄in) in from the sides and 2cm (³⁄₄in) up from the hem. Double-check that the first rod pocket is in the correct position. If necessary adjust the position of the lining.

13 Secure the lining to the interlining with horizontal rows of interlocking stitches at each rod pocket and halfway between each rod pocket at the fold line. Pin the sides of the lining to the blind and slip-stitch down each side and along the hem, taking care not to stitch through to the front of the blind.

14 To hold the fabric, lining and interlining together sew small 'spot tack' stitches through the three fabrics just on the fabric pocket machine lines, 10cm (4in) in from each end (see page 134). If your blind is wider than 60cm (24in) you will need to sew additional 'spot tacks' equally spaced no more than 35cm (14in) apart across the blind. If you match the colour of your thread to your fabric the stitching will be barely visible from the right side of the blind.

15 Working on the right side of the blind, measure up from the bottom of the hem to the finished length of the blind and mark the top with a row of pins. At the pin line fold over the remaining fabric to the back. Cut off the excess fabric to 1.5cm (⁵⁄₈in). Cut the loop Velcro to the finished width of the blind. With wrong side facing pin the Velcro to the top of the blind. Now machine the top, bottom and sides of the Velcro, ensuring you have concealed the raw edges of the fabric.

16 With a junior hacksaw cut the white plastic-coated weighted rod to the width of the blind minus 1cm (³⁄₈in). Fit the end caps to the rod, slide into the lowest pocket and hand-sew the side opening closed.

17 Still using the junior hacksaw cut the required number of fibreglass rods to the width of the blind minus 1cm (³⁄₈in). Take care at this point as fibreglass splinters, so make sure you wear protective gloves and wrap masking tape around the cutting area before cutting. If using protective plastic end caps, fit them at each end of the rods. Now slide the rods into the pockets and hand-sew the side openings closed.

18 With the hacksaw cut the bottom aluminium bar to the width of the blind less 2cm (³⁄₄in). Brush away any metal dust and fit the plastic end caps. Slide the bar through the gap at the mitred corner and stitch the mitres closed.

19 Sew the rings to the rod pockets 10cm (4in) in from each side. If your blind is wider than 60cm (24in) you will need to attach additional rings equally spaced approximately 35cm (14in) apart across the blind.

20 To complete your blind, follow the fitting instructions for your chosen headrail from pages 62–5.

Interlined blind before Velcro heading is attached.

BLACKOUT ROMAN BLINDS

It is possible, using blackout lining, or black Bolton twill as an interlining, to reduce the light shining through the blind.

Unfortunately, when using blackout lining light will still show though the tiny pin holes where the laminate has been pierced by stab stitches or machined sewing lines. Interlining your Roman blind with black Bolton twill will avoid this problem but the blind will take considerably more time to make up and may be heavier.

If you are using a light-coloured face fabric and wish to interline your blind with black Bolton twill, then you will also need an extra layer of cream domett interlining. Interlock this between the face fabric and the black Bolton twill to prevent the black fabric showing through to the front. This additional layer of interlining will, of course, increase the weight of your blind so a rotary chain lifting mechanism may be your best choice.

Note that whichever method you use, light will still show around the edges of the blind even when snuggly fitted in a recess.

Roman blind headrails

There are three types of lifting mechanisms for your Roman blind. When choosing one, think about your budget, the finished weight of the blind and your personal preferred method of lifting, in both manual and visual terms.

WOODEN BATTEN

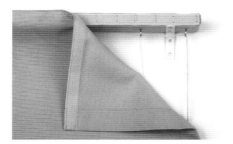

The least expensive lifting system is the traditional fabric-covered wooden batten with a series of cords, screw eyes and a wall-fixed cleat. The screw eyes are fixed to the underside of the batten to carry the draw cords. The cords are finished off with an acorn. When the blind is drawn up the cords are tied off on the cleat. Cleats are available in a wide range of finishes to suit your windows.

CORDED ALUMINIUM HEADRAIL

The corded lifting system comprises a headrail with moveable cord guides and a cord-locking device at one end. Clip-on universal wall brackets are attached to the track and can be moved as required. The headrail comes with hook Velcro already attached.

The cords are threaded through the rings on the back of your blind, then through the cord guides and cord-locking device at top of the headrail. The locking device means that you don't need a wall-fixed cleat. The individual cords can then be threaded into a cord connector so that only one cord is used to raise and lower the blind and hangs discreetly at the side.

You can buy this system as a kit for fitting your hand-made blinds. The headrail can be cut down in size with a junior hacksaw and the cord guides can be aligned to the rings on your blind as required.

ROTARY ALUMINIUM HEADRAIL

This is the most expensive of the three lifting systems but is also the most robust. Depending on quality, it can usually be used to lift blinds up to 5kg in weight. It comprises a headrail with moveable tape reels, a drive shaft and a rotary chain drive at one end. Clip-on universal wall brackets are attached to the track and can be moved as required. The headrail comes with hook Velcro already attached.

The blind is lifted by tapes, fitted into reels fixed to the top of the headrail and operated by a rotary chain drive. The tapes are attached to the bottom of the rod pocket behind with tape-locking clips. You can buy this system as a kit for fitting your hand-made blinds. Kits normally come with a loop of white plastic chain which will hang permanently at the side of the blind. This chain can usually be changed for brass or chrome, so follow the manufacturer's instructions on how to do this.

FITTING A ROMAN BLIND TO A WOODEN BATTEN

1 With a small wood saw, cut the wooden batten to the same width as the finished blind minus 1cm (³/₈in), and cover with matching fabric. Fold the fabric over the batten and staple in place, making sure the raw edges are hidden at the back of the batten.

2 Cut a length of hook Velcro to the same width as the batten and secure to the front of the batten with staples.

3 Lay the batten along the top edge of the blind and mark the position of the cords. Insert a large screw eye at each mark on the underside of the batten. Make sure the screw eye is side on. With the Velcro facing you, fit an additional screw eye at the right-hand end of the batten if you want a right-hand-operating blind. The reverse applies if you want a left-hand-operating blind.

4 Screw your angle brackets to either the inside or outside of the window recess as appropriate. Screw the batten to the brackets.

5 To hang the blind, align the loop Velcro on the blind to the hook Velcro on the batten and firmly press in place. Make sure your blind is fitted squarely.

6 Tie a length of blind cord to the lowest ring and thread through all the rings up to the screw eye, through the other screw eyes along the batten and down the side. Repeat for all the remaining rings.

7 Lower the blind, gather the cords hanging at the side of the blind and apply a little tension to each cord to take out any slack. Cut the ends level and thread through the acorn. Tie the cords into a knot and hide the ends inside the acorn.

8 Fix the cleat onto the wall at an easily accessible height.

9 Pull up the blind, helping it into its folds, and wrap the cords around the cleat to secure the blind. The fabric will need time to 'dress' into folds, so leave the blind drawn up for a couple of days. After this time it should easily pleat up into neat folds.

10 If the blind does not pull up evenly or hang level or it swings to one side, then check that it is sitting level on the batten and also that the draw cords are evenly tensioned.

Blind cord with a wooden acorn, wound round a cleat

Professional tip

The quickest way we have found of tying a secure knot for Roman blind cords is to:

1 Tie a small loop at the end of the cord. Cut off any excess cord.

2 Push the loop through the blind ring.

3 Then push the other end of the cord through the loop and pull tight.

FITTING A ROMAN BLIND TO A CORDED ALUMINIUM HEADRAIL

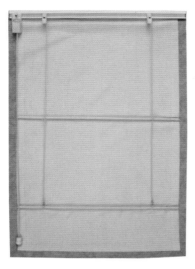

1   If required, cut the headrail to the width of the blind minus 1cm (³/₈in), using a junior hacksaw, and brush away any metal dust.

2   Space the wall brackets evenly across the headrail. Make sure they do not coincide with the cord guides or cord lock. Mark the fixing position of the brackets on the wall. The universal brackets can be face-fixed to the outside of the window reveal or top-fixed inside the reveal. Unclip the brackets from the headrail by depressing the tab lock underneath and screw the brackets in place.

3   The kit will come ready to operate at the right-hand side. If you wish to change the operation, just remove both headrail end caps (if fitted), unscrew the cord lock and move it to the other side of the headrail. Replace the two end caps.

4   It is easier to fit the blind to the headrail before fitting the headrail onto the brackets. Lay the blind face down and align the loop tape already attached to the back of the blind to the hook tape on the headrail. Make sure your blind is fitted squarely.

5   Thread the cord through the left-hand cord guide and down through the rings. Knot it to the bottom ring and make sure it is secure. Trim the free end close to the knot. Repeat the threading for the right-hand cord guide and any additional cord guides.

6   Clip the headrail and blind onto the brackets.

7   To ensure all the cords are equally tensioned pull the cords tight and thread through the acorn. Tie the cords together and feed the knot back into the acorn.

8   To lock the blind at the desired height, pull the cords towards you and release gently.

9   To release the cords, pull the cords straight down and release gently.

Step 7

Professional tip

Wide blinds will have a lot of cords. To tidy these, use a cord connector. To fit the connector:

1 Ensure all the cords are equally tensioned, pull the cords tight and tie them together.

2 With the blinds in the down position trim the ends 15cm (6in) below the cord lock.

3 Open the cord connector, insert the multiple cords into one half and the single cord into the other. Adjust the length of the single cord with the cord weight.

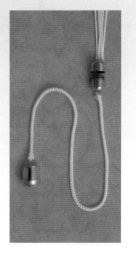

YOU WILL NEED
Unlined, lined or interlined
Roman blind
Corded headrail kit
Scissors
Junior hacksaw
Tool kit for fitting

FITTING A ROMAN BLIND TO A ROTARY CHAIN ALUMINIUM HEADRAIL

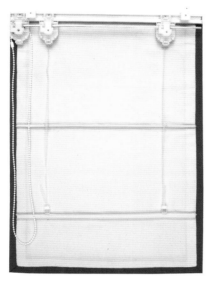

1   If required, cut the headrail to the width of the blind minus 1cm (³⁄₈in), using a junior hacksaw, and brush away any metal dust. Cut the rotary chain drive shaft 2cm (³⁄₄in) shorter than the headrail.

2   Space the wall brackets evenly across the headrail. Make sure their position does not coincide with the tape reels or the chain drive. Mark the fixing position of the brackets on the wall. The universal brackets can be face-fixed to the outside of the window reveal or top-fixed inside the reveal. Unclip the brackets from the headrail by depressing the tab lock underneath and screw the brackets in place.

3   The kit will come ready to operate at the right-hand side. If you wish to change the operation, just remove both headrail end caps (if fitted), unscrew the rotary chain device and move it to the other side of the headrail. Replace the two end caps.

4   It is easier to fit the blind to the headrail before fitting the headrail onto the brackets. Lay the blind face down and align the loop tape already attached to the back of the blind to the hook tape on the headrail. Make sure your blind is fitted squarely.

5   The tapes will usually come already fitted to the tape housing. Feed the tapes down through each of the rings to the penultimate ring. Rotary chain kits normally come with a tape-locking clip, so secure your tape to this and clip it to the bottom ring. Tension the tapes evenly.

6   Clip the blind onto the brackets and pull the blind up to see if the tapes are equally tensioned. If necessary, adjust the length of the tape using the tape-locking clip.

Professional tip

To attach the tape through the tape-locking clip:

1   Take the tape-locking clip and thread the tape through the top, around the bottom bar and back out of the top.

2   Make sure you have a long end of tape coming out of the top.

3   Grasp the two loops of tape and tug firmly upwards; the device will self-lock. Make sure it is secure.

YOU WILL NEED
Roman blind
Rotary chain headrail kit
Scissors
Junior hacksaw
Tool kit for fitting

Roman blind design details

Borders need to be sewn onto the main fabric before you start making the blind. They can be made from the same fabric in a different colourway, or a contrasting fabric. Whatever your choice, make sure its weight is compatible with that of the main fabric, to avoid getting puckered seams.

Decide on which borders you want – bottom, side or both. Now decide the width of the borders: these are usually between 2.5cm and 10cm (1–4in).

When estimating and cutting fabric for your border allow the width of the border plus a 2cm (³⁄₄in) seam allowance, plus 4cm (1¹⁄₂in) for turning allowances.

For the length of the border allow the cut length of the blind, plus approximately 20cm (8in).

Each border should be made from one single length of fabric which matches the cut length or width of your blind. This is because you want to avoid unsightly seams across the border at all costs.

1   Before starting on your blind, first establish the finished size. See page 41 for how to do this.

2   Decide on the headrail. See page 62 for details.

3   Calculate your rod pocket spacing and number of folds. Use one of the methods on pages 48–53.

4   Decide on which borders and what widths you want.

5   To prevent your fabrics from shrinking once made up, it is advisable to steam the two fabrics with an iron before cutting and sewing them together.

6   Cut the main fabric to the finished measurements of the blind, minus the bottom and side border widths, but still add a 2cm (³⁄₄in) seam allowance to each side which will have a border. You must also add 4cm (1¹⁄₂in) to the length for a top turning allowance.

7   Cut the lower edge border 40cm (16in) longer than the main fabric to allow for the mitred corners and seam allowances. Cut the length of the side edges 20cm (8in) longer than the main fabric. Any excess fabric can be trimmed at a later point. Borders wider than 10cm (4in) will need longer strips.

8   On the main fabric, you need to identify the corners where the seams of the borders will meet. At each bottom corner, measure up 2cm (³⁄₄in) and in 2cm (³⁄₄in) and mark this point with a pin. This will be the corner point where the stitch lines attaching your borders will meet.

9   Place the lower edge border against the main fabric, right sides of the fabrics together. Machine accurately a 2cm (³⁄₄in) seam from corner point to corner point.

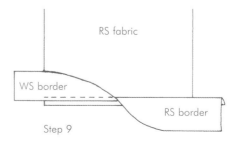

RS fabric

WS border

RS border

Step 9

10 To seam the side borders to the main fabric, place the first side border against the main fabric, right sides together and lined up at the top. Machine accurately a 2cm (³⁄₄in) seam from the top of the blind to the corner point. Repeat for the other side panel.

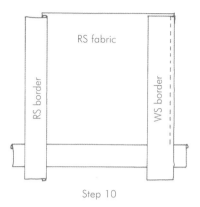

Step 10

11 With the right side of the blind uppermost fold each border underneath at 45° to make the mitre, and press.

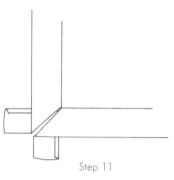

Step 11

12 With right sides together seam along the creased mitre. Press the seam open. Trim away any excess fabric.

13 Repeat for the other corner.

Now follow steps **5–17** given for the lined Roman blind.

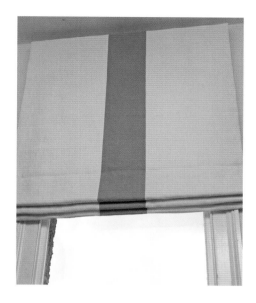

MAKING ROMAN BLINDS WITH INSET PANELS

Inset panels can be 5 to 30cm (2–12in) in width. This type of blind can also be interlined. Seam your panels to your main fabric, pressing the seams so that they fall behind the darker of the two fabrics and then follow the make-up method for your preferred blind.

TRIMMINGS

If you want to have flat braids on your blind, these need be machined onto your fabric before you start making the blind. It is a good idea to steam-iron the blind fabric and your braids to minimise any differential shrinkage.

Trimmings and fringes for the lower edge can be sewn on by hand after the blinds has been made.

YOU WILL NEED

Fabric and contrast fabric
See lined Roman blinds for
remaining components

Curtains

"Curtains bring softness and warmth to a room"

Curtains

Full-length curtains look elegant, they also give visual height and bring warmth to any room.

In their most basic form curtains are gathered or pleated panels of fabric, hung from tracks or poles at windows, for privacy and insulation against noise and draughts.

Usually hung in pairs, curtains soften the edges of windows. Curtains can be any length from just below the sill to full length, depending on the situation. Very few curtains are fitted inside the recess.

Sill length is practical in kitchens and bathrooms but full-length curtains will look more elegant in main living rooms.

Curtains can be combined with most blinds and often will make blinds look less austere.

An often-overlooked opportunity, curtains bring texture and pattern into a room. They also make a room inviting and at night they can make a room feel very cosy.

Lots of factors need to be considered to make your curtains look good. Firstly, decide whether to have your curtains unlined, lined or interlined. Then choose a heading that suits your room style. Tape headings, clips, eyelets, tabs, or even hand-sewn headings are all available options. Fitting and hanging your curtains is the final step.

If you wish to make an individual statement for your home, then follow our step-by-step instructions to make beautiful hand-made curtains that will afford years of pleasure.

Left and right Overlong curtains with a pin-hooked pleated heading made from a contrast fabric.

Unlined curtains and sheer curtains are made up in exactly the same way and can be hand-sewn or machined.

Sheer curtains have wonderful translucent qualities, filtering natural light without screening any of the view.

They can be used in rooms which require privacy during the day but need to allow the light to filter in.

Ease of care for sheers is important in cities, where they are the first defence against dirt and grime.

Sheers come in a variety of patterns, textured weaves and colours. Many sheers come in wide widths which means there is no need to join them with unsightly seams, which would show against the daylight.

Unlined curtains can be soft and pretty, allowing light to filter in and brighten your rooms.

Unlined cotton curtains combine well with blinds as they soften hard edges. However, they won't insulate the room in the same way as lined or interlined curtains, or absorb as much noise.

As the light shines through, unlined curtains show off patterned fabrics and highlight colours.

For people who like to ring the changes, these curtains are quick, simple and relatively inexpensive to make. Unlined curtains can also be washed, making them very practical.

Left   Layered sheer curtains.
Right   Unlined curtains hung behind lined curtains.

"Unlined curtains are light and summery"

Lining and interlining protects the main fabric and improves the drape of curtains.

Lining is a smooth sateen-woven cotton fabric, which is the first defence against the sun and dirt. Better-quality linings have a sun-resistant finish to them. If the curtains are likely to be up for any length of time, then it's worth getting the sun-resistant linings. Coloured linings and blackout linings are also available.

Some linings also have crease-resistant qualities. This will save a lot of time ironing if you're making them yourself.

Interlining your curtains makes them hang beautifully and look very impressive. Interlining is a blanket-type fabric which is sandwiched between the lining and the main fabric. Curtains can be lined with medium or heavyweight interlinings depending on how thick you want the curtains to look. Traditional interlinings are cotton but synthetic ones are also available. Whichever interlining you choose, always buy a pre-shrunk one.

Curtains which are lined or interlined should always be dry-cleaned.

Interlined curtains are very heavy and need to be hung on substantial poles or tracks.

Left   Coloured lining co-ordinates with the curtain fabric.

"Interlining makes curtains look really sumptuous"

Borders can often add drama to curtains.

Borders can be sewn onto the leading edges, bottoms and even the tops of curtains. Outside edges are not, as a rule, bordered.

It can also be a way of recycling older curtains, either by updating them and bringing them into your colour scheme with a fabric that matches your new colours, or lengthening or widening them for new windows.

For deep borders, let the architecture in your room suggest where you place them. Consider aligning hem borders with skirting boards or window edges to create a contemporary look.

Left   A plain border accentuates the leading edges of these curtains.

Right   A deep hem border of the same fabric in a different colourway.

"Borders accentuate the edges of curtains"

Trimmings can soften the leading edges of curtains.

You can personalise both ready-made and hand-sewn curtains with well-chosen embellishments.

Carefully chosen trimmings add interest to plain curtains.

Emphasise curtain hems and edges or fabric design details with decorative trims and edgings.

Trimmings can look very stylish and bring added texture into a room. They are an opportunity to be creative and bring additional detail to your scheme.

Left and right Bead trimmings inset into the leading edges complement the curtain fabrics.

Curtain headings

Gathered heading tape is the standard way to head unlined, lined or interlined curtains.

The tape is machined at or near the top of the curtain and pulled with a series of cords to form the gathers. The cords are tied off, or wrapped around a cord tidy, when the curtains are the required width.

Metal or plastic hooks are inserted into loops on the back of the tape to hang the curtain on a track or pole.

Gathered heading tape comes in varying widths; 2.5cm (1in) tapes look quite casual while the wider 15cm (6in) tapes look more formal.

Some heading tapes are softer than others, so for a crisp finish you will need to choose a stiffer tape.

To avoid machine lines, hand-sew your heading tape to your curtains. This will give a very smart finish and although it is time-consuming the result can be very pleasing.

When hanging tape-headed curtains allow plenty of time for drawing up the cords and dressing the curtain into even folds, particularly when windows are wide.

Left Interlined curtains with 7.5cm (3in) gathered tape heading, held back with rope tiebacks.

Right 2.5cm (1in) gathered heading tape sewn at the bottom of the contrasting flop-over frill heading.

Tab-headed curtains are economical on fabric.

The flat curtain panel has tabs spaced equally along the top edge. For tab headings you only need one and a half times fullness of fabric.

Tabs in modern materials like leather and suede can be easily bought, or you can make fabric tabs in matching or contrasting fabric. If you choose a very thick pole, then you will need to make or buy longer tabs.

Fabric tabs do not slide along the pole terribly well, so are best suited for situations where the curtain is not being constantly drawn.

Right and below Brown leather tabs with snap metal rivets are distinctive on these overlong curtains.

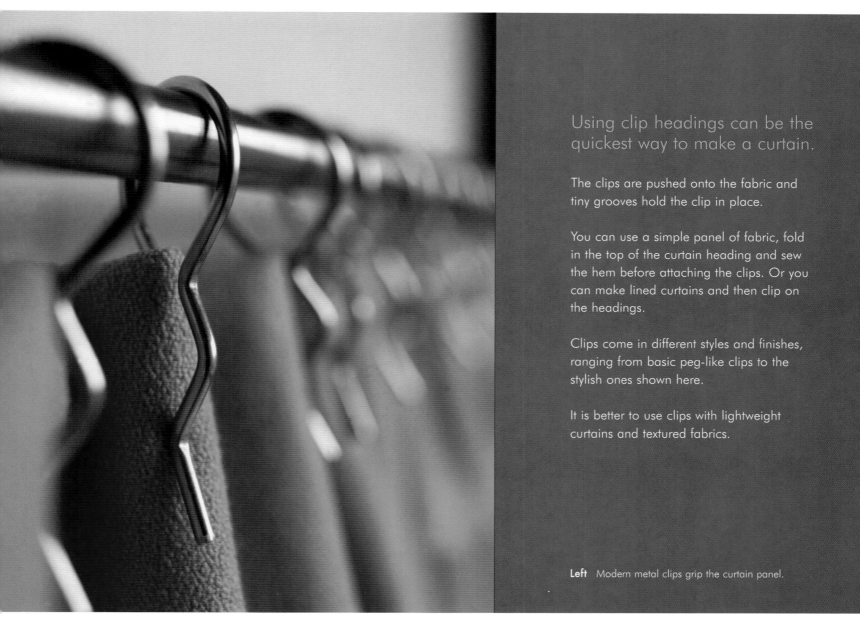

Using clip headings can be the quickest way to make a curtain.

The clips are pushed onto the fabric and tiny grooves hold the clip in place.

You can use a simple panel of fabric, fold in the top of the curtain heading and sew the hem before attaching the clips. Or you can make lined curtains and then clip on the headings.

Clips come in different styles and finishes, ranging from basic peg-like clips to the stylish ones shown here.

It is better to use clips with lightweight curtains and textured fabrics.

Left Modern metal clips grip the curtain panel.

"Clip headings are popular with young homemakers"

Eyelet-headed curtains are gaining popularity.

First seen in the 1950s, eyelets are back in fashion in today's homes. The use of unusual fabrics, such as faux suede and synthetic taffetas, has given this retro curtain heading a modern slant.

Metal or plastic eyelets are pressed into the fabric and then threaded over the pole before it is put onto its brackets.

The eyelets encourage the curtain fabric to hang in neatly defined folds, creating a sleek and streamlined look. Even when closed at night, these curtains are not fully flat, maintaining a series of attractive shallow folds.

Bordered curtains suit eyelet headings particularly well.

Curtain eyelets come in a range of metallic finishes as well as colours.

The internal diameter of the eyelet needs to be 2cm ($^{3}/_{4}$in) larger than the diameter of your pole so that the curtains can move easily.

The simple design of the eyelet curtain belies the sometimes involved make-up process. Hand tools and small eyelets can be bought from some DIY stores.

Large eyelets will need to be pressed in place using a professional eyelet press. Specialist companies offer an eyeleting service for made-up curtain panels.

The simplest eyelet heading is to sew eyelet heading tape to the back of the curtain.

"Eyelet headings are simple and sleek"

Hand-pleating allows you to choose where you place your pleats.

Curtains which have been hand-pleated will hang in an orderly column-like fashion and emphasise the height of your room.

A major benefit is that on patterned fabrics you can choose where to have your pleats so that they follow the horizontal pattern repeat. This makes the curtains very pleasing to the eye. Careful planning will ensure success when pleating patterned fabrics.

There are a wide variety of pleated headings.

French headings are also known as triple pleats as each pleat is folded into three and sewn in place at the bottom of the pleat. This heading stacks back neatly, allowing the maximum amount of light into a room.

Left French-headed curtains, with an inset border along the leading edge and hem, hung from a glass pole.

Goblet headings are so named because the pleat is shaped like a wine goblet.

Box pleating is where a single pleat is flattened. This heading is best used on dress or fix-headed curtains as it does not stack back very easily.

For inverted-pleat headings a single pleat is taken to the back of the curtain and secured, resulting in a very modern-looking heading.

Tête de Versailles is a single pleat which is created in the opposite way to an inverted-pleat heading as the pleat is brought forward. Again this looks modern.

The simplest of all is the pin-hooked heading. The hooks are used to form the pleat. Two hooks are placed in the glider at the same time, causing the curtain to balloon out in attractive folds (see page 70). As it is not sewn into place, it is not as robust as the other headings.

Right Inverted-pleat headings for dress curtains hung from a thick wooden pole.

"Hand-pleating creates orderly and elegant curtains"

Hand pleats are created by inserting a stiffened fabric, known as buckram, into the top of the curtain. The heading is hand-pleated and sewn in place.

Hooks are either hand-sewn or pinned into the buckram at the back of the curtain heading.

If you do not wish to go to the effort of hand-pleating, you can buy specialised curtain tapes available for French, goblet and box pleats. The pleating effect is created by drawing cords on the tapes, but the effect is not as smart as hand-pleating.

Opposite page Box-pleated curtains.
This page Goblet-headed curtains.

Curtain fittings

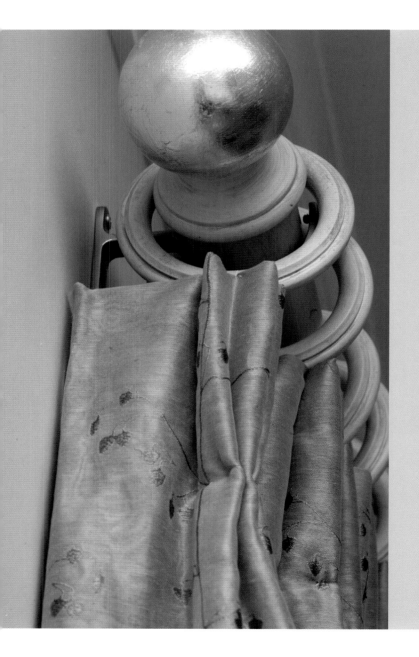

There are two main ways to hang curtains; on tracks or on poles.

Curtain tracks tend to be functional rather than decorative, so benefit from being concealed by a fabric-covered lath where possible.

Curtain poles are decorative as well as functional curtain fittings. The final flourish for a pole is a finial on the end.

The choice of poles has increased dramatically, ranging from the traditional wood, iron and brass to the contemporary satin nickel and even glass.

Wooden poles tend to come in 25mm (1in), 35mm (1½in), 50mm (2in) and 63mm (2½in) diameters. They can be stained, painted or even gilded. Finials range from just simple balls ends to being elaborately carved. For heavier curtains, choose a substantial pole and fixings.

Metal poles usually come in 19mm (¾in) and 32mm (1¼in), again with a range of finishes and finials.

Left French-headed curtains, hung from a painted wooden pole with a silver ball end finial. The outside edge of the curtain has been returned to the wall.

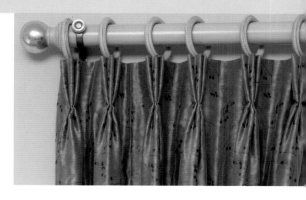

A fabric-covered lath is a narrow fabric-covered pelmet which hides the curtain track behind.

The fascia of a fabric-covered lath is made from either buckram or hardboard and covered with the curtain fabric. The depth of the fascia needs to just cover the track so that the gliders and curtain hooks move freely behind.

It is simple but smart treatment which can be fitted to large or small windows and works well in modern or traditional settings.

They are a good choice when ceilings are low and there is little or no space above the window.

It is best to choose a French heading when using laths as the curtains then stack back compactly.

Left   French-headed curtains, hung from a fabric-covered lath.

"A discreet way of concealing curtain tracks"

Curtain essentials and make-up

This section covers the practical issues surrounding curtains and curtain making: choosing curtain fittings and measuring them; estimating fabric; making unlined, lined and interlined curtains with a range of curtain headings; and hanging curtains.

There are no rigid rules for curtain making. The methods described in this section have been devised over the years in our workroom. If you are new to sewing then follow our instructions and remember that lack of experience can almost always be compensated for with patience and by allowing yourself plenty of time. If you are a more experienced curtain maker, then you may prefer to adapt our methods to suit the way you work.

CHOOSING TRACKS, POLES AND FABRIC-COVERED LATHS

Decide whether you wish to hang your curtains from a pole, a fabric-covered lath or a track. For curtain fittings see pages 88 and 89.

If you wish to have a track, use plastic ones for light to mediumweight curtains (most unlined and lined curtains). For medium to heavyweight curtains (lined and interlined curtains) use metal tracks. Tracks are functional rather than decorative and ideally should be covered with a top treatment or a fabric-covered lath.

For tracks, you can choose to have them corded or uncorded. If choosing a corded track also think about whether you want left- or right-hand pulls. Corded tracks come with cord tensioners which need to be fixed to the wall or skirting. Alternatively, for windows that are taller than they are wide, you can use brass acorn weights.

LENGTH OF TRACK OR POLE

Measure the width of the window and extend the track or pole, excluding the finials, by 20 to 35cm (8–14in) either side of the window. This will allow the curtains to stack back against the wall and maximise the light coming into the room.

POSITION OF TRACK OR POLE

Tracks and laths can be face- or ceiling-fixed. Poles can be face-fixed, recess-fixed or ceiling-fixed with appropriate brackets. The curtain fitting should be fixed level with the window frame or 10 to 20cm (4–8in) above the window. For tab-headed curtains, fit the pole approximately 15cm (6in) above the top of the window to minimise light coming through the space between the tabs.

FITTING POLES

Fit pole brackets 5cm (2in) in from each end of the pole, excluding finials. One ring is placed on the outside of each bracket, and the remaining rings are placed between. Use the same number of rings as curtain hooks. Remove excess rings. Poles over 2.4 metres (94in) will always need a supporting centre bracket, in which case you need an equal number of rings on each side of the centre bracket.

Professional tip

If there is a radiator below the window, or a face-fixed blind already fitted, you may need to project your curtain fitting out from the wall. Extension brackets can be bought for poles, or you can make the pelmet board supporting your fabric-covered lath deeper (see page 112).

MEASURING FOR CURTAINS

It is well worth allowing yourself time to measure accurately; don't rush it. Measure with a steel tape measure rather than a fabric one as the latter can stretch over time. Take your measurements in either metric or Imperial – don't mix the two. If you decide to measure in metric then use one standard, either millimetres or centimetres. Finally, the best advice we can give you is to always double-check your measurements and make a careful note of them all.

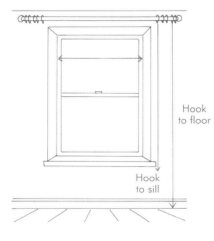

MEASURING CURTAIN FITTINGS

If not already in place, fix your chosen curtain fitting and then measure for your curtains.

Measure the length of the track or pole, excluding finials.

Decide on whether you want your curtains to finish on the sill, just below the sill, to the floor, or if you want them to be overlong.

Measure from the eye of the glider or the eye on the pole ring to where you want the curtain to finish. This is your 'hook drop' and will determine where your hook will be placed on the back of the curtain. For tracks, also measure from the top of the track to where you want the curtain to finish. This will be the finished length of your curtain.

For eyelet and tab-headed curtains measure from the top of the pole to where you want your curtain to finish.

If your floor is uneven, take three measurements across the fitting. To disguise the unevenness you can also consider making your curtains overlong by 1 to 10cm (⅜–4in).

FINDING THE FINISHED CURTAIN WIDTH

For a pair of curtains, take the width of your curtain fitting, add 7cm (2¾in) for overlap plus 2cm (¾in) for every 50cm (20in) of track or pole length for ease.

If you are going to return your curtains to the wall, as per the Professional Tip below, also add your two returns.

Then divide this number by two to obtain the finished width of each curtain.

FINDING THE FINISHED CURTAIN LENGTH AND HOOK POSITION

For curtains hung from a pole, take the hook drop and add 2cm (¾in) so that the curtain hook is covered. This is your finished curtain length. For 19mm (¾in) poles you might only need 1cm (⅜in) to cover the hook.

For curtains hung from a track, the finished length of your curtains is the measurement from the top of the track to where you want the curtain to finish. To establish the hook position, measure down from the top of the track to the eye of the glider.

For curtains hung from a fabric-covered lath, the finished length is the measurement from the top of the lath to where you want the curtain to finish. To establish the hook position, measure down from the top of the track to the eye of the glider.

For eyelet curtains measure from the top of the pole to where you want the curtain to finish and add 3.5cm (1¼in).

For tab-headed curtains measure from the top of the pole to where you want the curtain to finish. This is the measurement of the curtain including tabs.

> ### Professional tip
>
> *Professional curtain makers 'return' their curtains to the wall. See the picture on page 88.*
>
> *To close the gap between the end of your curtain and the wall, you need to allow extra width to each curtain. Measure how far your fitting projects from the wall to the eye of the glider or the eye of the pole ring. This is your return measurement.*

ESTIMATING FABRIC QUANTITIES FOR CURTAINS

To estimate how much fabric you will need for curtains, you need the length of your track or pole and also the finished length of your curtains. If your track or pole is not in place, then measure the width and drop roughly, but generously, so that you are not short of fabric. The fabric shop will need these measurements if they are estimating fabric for you.

Curtains are not flat panels, they all have fullness in them. The longer the track or pole, the more widths of fabric you will need for your curtains. Some headings will need less fullness than others. As a general rule curtains need 2 to 2½ times fullness. Clip and tab headings may only need 1½ times fullness.

NUMBER OF FABRIC WIDTHS REQUIRED

To accurately estimate how many widths of fabric you need, measure the length of the track or pole, add 7cm (2¾in) for overlap, plus 20cm (8in) for returns (if required), plus 2cm (¾in) for every 50cm (20in) of track or pole for ease: then multiply by the curtain fullness required. Divide the resultant figure by the width of the fabric. Round this figure up or down to the nearest whole number. This will give you the number of widths required.

To quickly calculate how many widths of fabric you need to buy use the table below, which allows for approximately 2 to 2½ times fullness.

NUMBER OF FABRIC WIDTHS REQUIRED FOR 2–2½ TIMES FULLNESS CURTAINS	
LENGTH RANGE OF TRACK, POLE OR FABRIC-COVERED LATH	NUMBER OF FABRIC WIDTHS REQUIRED (based on 137cm (54in) wide fabric)
120–160cm (48–63in)	3
150–230cm (60–90in)	4
220–300cm (86–118in)	5
280–360cm (110–141in)	6
330–430cm (130–169in)	7
390–500cm (154–197in)	8

ESTABLISHING THE CUT DROP

The cut drop is the finished length of your curtains plus an allowance for headings and hems. In our workroom, we allow 30cm (12in) for heading and hem allowances. Pressed eyelet headings require a 10cm (4in) heading allowance.

ESTIMATING TOTAL FABRIC QUANTITIES FOR PLAIN FABRICS

Simply multiply the number of fabric widths by the cut drop and round up to the nearest half width.

ESTIMATING TOTAL FABRIC QUANTITIES FOR PATTERNED FABRICS

So that the pattern on your curtain matches at the seams, the top of the cut drop needs to start at the same part of the pattern for every width.

Ask the fabric shop for the pattern repeat. Divide the cut drop by the pattern repeat and round up the resultant figure to the nearest whole number. Multiply this whole number by the length of the pattern repeat. This gives the adjusted cut drop.

To calculate your total fabric quantity, multiply the adjusted cut drop by the number of widths of fabric required, then add one extra pattern repeat and round up to the nearest half width. The extra pattern repeat allows you to choose where on the pattern your curtain starts.

EXAMPLE

Number of widths required = 3
Finished length = 230cm, pattern repeat = 18cm
Heading and hem allowance = 30cm

230cm + 30cm = 260cm cut drop

260cm ÷ 18cm = 14.44
Round this up to 15

15 x 18cm = 270cm adjusted cut drop

(3 widths x 270cm) +18cm = 8.28m fabric

Round up to 8.5 metres to obtain the total fabric required.

LINING AND INTERLINING

Calculate as for plain fabrics. Work out the amounts in the same way as the main fabric but only add 20cm (8in) for heading and hem allowances.

NOTE ABOUT FABRIC WIDTHS

Most fabrics, linings and interlinings come in widths of 137cm (54in). However, some silks come in widths of 120cm (48in) and some cottons come in widths of 150cm (60in). Also, modern machinery can produce some fabrics in wider widths of 280cm (110in) and 300cm (118in).

If you are using widths other than 137cm, then do not use the table opposite left to calculate the number of fabric widths required. Use the calculation method described instead.

SHEERS

Sheer curtains need 2 to 3 times fullness.

Sheer fabrics can come in very wide widths so there may be no need to join them.

Add 20cm (8in) to the curtain length for heading and hem allowances.

Some sheer fabrics are already weighted at the hem, in which case just add 7.5cm (3in) for the top turning allowance.

Buckram-headed sheer curtains need a heading and hem allowance of 20cm (8in) plus 2 x buckram depth.

CUTTING FABRICS

1   Calculate the cut drop by adding a heading and hem allowance to the finished length. See page 92 for adjusting the cut drop for patterned fabrics.

2   Check that you recognise the right and wrong sides of the fabric and as soon as you have finished cutting each drop, mark the top of the length and the right side of the fabric with a fabric marker.

3   Always cut out the fabric using a metal ruler and a L or set square. This will ensure your curtain will hang straight. Hold the ruler firm and with a fabric marker, draw right across the width below it.

4   Before cutting linings and interlinings, check that they are the same width as the fabric; if not, you will have to cut more, or less, to match up with the total width of your face fabric.

5   Ideally you should cut each length of fabric or lining from the same batch, as colours do vary.

6   The cut panels of fabric are joined together with a plain seam.

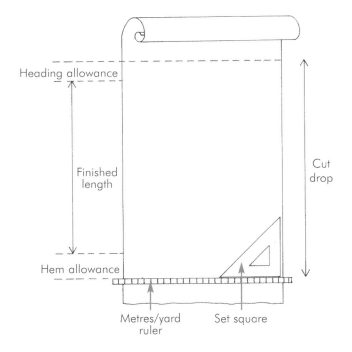

Heading allowance

Finished length

Hem allowance

Cut drop

Metres/yard ruler

Set square

PLAIN SEAMS

Most fabrics need a narrow 2cm (¾in) seam allowance.

Thicker, loosely woven fabrics may need a wider seam allowance.

Place the cut fabric panels right sides together and machine a line of stitching, taking the necessary seam allowance.

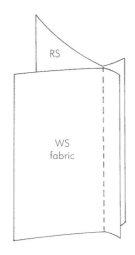

SEAMING WIDTHS OF FABRIC TOGETHER

When you have an uneven number of widths for your curtains, cut one width in half and seam half to each outside edge of the curtain.

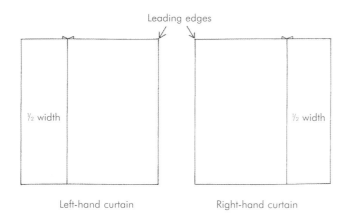

Left-hand curtain   Right-hand curtain

SEAMING WIDTHS OF PATTERNED FABRIC

Surprisingly we have found the easiest way to match up widths of patterned fabrics is to do it while seated at the sewing machine rather than spending time pinning and tacking.

1   Place two fabric panels right sides together and align the pattern.

2   Work on a 10cm (4in) section at a time. Fold back the seam allowance on the top piece of fabric.

3   Accurately match the pattern and make a crease line.

4   Hold the fabric in place, turn the seam allowance back to meet the bottom fabric and machine down the crease line.

5   Repeat in 10cm (4in) sections until you have machined down the whole length. Any minor mismatched sections can be unpicked later and remachined.

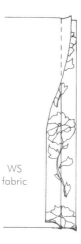

PREPARING LININGS

1   Cut out the lining.

2   Machine the lining panels, right sides together, using plain seams.

3   Press the seams open.

4   If working with an odd number of widths, remember to seam half widths onto the outer side of each curtain lining.

5   Fold up the hem 7.5cm (3in) and press. Fold up the same amount again, and pin in place, ready to machine.

6   A quick way to press up the hem without measuring is to cut a strip of card 7.5cm (3in) deep, over which the fabric is folded. Slip the card out, pin and machine.

PREPARING INTERLININGS

Interlining can be joined using a plain seam but an overlapped seam is flat and less bulky. Overlap selvedges 1.5cm (⅝in) and machine together.

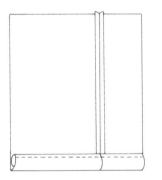

Seamed and hemmed lining

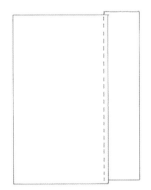

Overlap-seamed interlining

CHAIN-STITCHING LININGS TO HEMS

1   Start with a long piece of thread brought through from the back of the lining.

2   Make a big loop around the first three fingers of your left hand, holding the thread taut in your right hand. You can take the needle off, or let it lie at the other end of the thread.

3   Reach through the loop with your left fingers to catch the taut thread and pull it back through the loop, tightening gently until the chain stitch is formed.

4   Repeat until the chain is approximately 2.5cm (1in) long. You will now have a length of very strong chain stitch. To tie it off, thread the needle through the loop and pull. Secure the end to the hem of the fabric.

5   A chain every half width will make sure your lining and fabric hang together professionally.

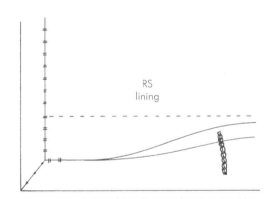

RS
lining

Finished chain linking fabric hem and underside of lining

Making sheer and unlined curtains

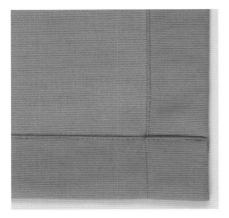

An unlined curtain with a machined corner

This is a good first curtain project to start on. The side turnings and hems can either be machined or hand-sewn.

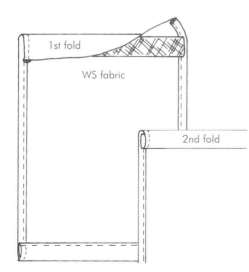

MACHINING UNLINED CURTAINS

1   Establish the number of fabric widths required, the finished length and the cut drop of your curtains (see page 92).

2   Cut out your fabric and seam the widths together (see page 94).

3   Fold in the side edges 4cm (1½in) and fold over a further 4cm (1½in). Pin in place and machine along the folded edge.

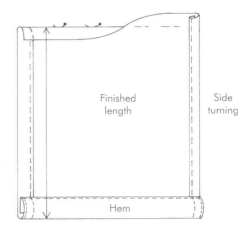

4   Fold up the hem 8cm (3in) and fold up again 8cm (3in). Pin in place and machine the hem.

5   Measure the finished length up from the hem and mark with a line of pins. Transfer the pins to the right side. Fold over the top of the curtain, level with the pins. The raw edges will be covered by the heading tape.

6   Follow the instructions for tape headings on page 102.

YOU WILL NEED

Fabric
Heading tape
Sewing kit

Making lined curtains

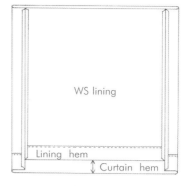

Steps 1–5

The method we have shown you here is for a machine-made lined curtain. If you want to make a hand-sewn lined curtain, then follow the instructions for an interlined curtain, but omit the stages relating to the insertion of the interlining.

MACHINING LINED CURTAINS

1   Establish the number of fabric widths required, the finished length and the cut drop of your curtains (see page 92).

2   Prepare your lining (see page 95). Cut out your main fabric and seam the widths together (see page 94).

3   Fold up the hem 12cm (5in) and fold over 12cm (5in) again. Pin in place and machine.

4   Trim the outside edge of the lining, so that the panel measures 8cm (3in) less than the curtain fabric.

5   Place the lining onto the curtain fabric, 4cm (1½in) up from the hem, right sides together. Machine up each side, taking a 2cm (¾in) seam allowance.

6   Turn the curtain through to the right side. Press 4cm (1½in) of fabric over onto the wrong side of the curtain at each side, so that the lining lies flat.

7   To neaten the raw edges at the hem, fold up and into the sides to neaten. Slip-stitch in place.

8   Measure the finished length up from the hem, and mark it with a line of pins. Transfer the pins to the right side of the fabric. Fold over the top at the pin line.

9   Follow the instructions for your chosen heading (see pages 102, 108–11).

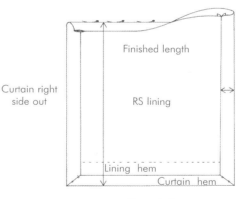

Steps 6–8

YOU WILL NEED

Fabric
Lining
Sewing kit

Making interlined curtains

An interlined curtain has a soft extra layer 'sandwiched' between the fabric and lining. Interlining makes curtains look sumptuous and drape beautifully, as well as absorbing sound and providing insulation.

Interlining a curtain is an advanced make-up technique and is not recommended as a first sewing project. It involves more sewing than making unlined or lined curtains.

Choose a medium or heavyweight interlining, such as pre-shrunk domett (260g/m²) or bump (410g/m²). Alternatively you can use a synthetic interlining called sarril (either 180g/m² or 220g/m²).

Any interlining has to be stitched to the main fabric and the lining so that the three fabrics drape as one. Interlining will increase the weight of your curtains significantly.

Also available is a time-saving combined lining and interlining, which is a sarril fused to a sateen or blackout lining. You can follow these make-up instructions and omit the steps relating to inserting separate interlining, or follow the instructions for a machined lined curtain instead. Using it will reduce the make-up time, but the resulting curtain will not drape as well.

HAND-SEWING INTERLINED CURTAINS

1   Establish the number of widths of fabric required, the finished length and the cut drop of your curtains (see page 92).

2   Prepare your lining and interlining (see page 95). Cut out your main fabric and seam the widths together (see page 94).

3   Lay the interlining onto the wrong side of the fabric, placing the side edges together. Place the interlining 12cm (5in) up from the lower edge. Smooth out the interlining so that it is completely flat.

4   Carefully fold back the interlining lengthways and interlock to the fabric every quarter width, half width, at the seams and 15cm (6in) in from the side edges (see page 134). Always work the interlocking stitch from the hem upwards and stop 25cm (10in) from the top of the curtain.

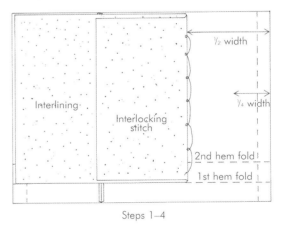

Steps 1–4

5   Mitre the corners of the hem and insert fabric-covered weights (see page opposite).

6   Fold over the 6cm (2¼in) side turning allowance and herringbone-stitch to the interlining, stopping 25cm (10in) from the top of the curtain.

> **YOU WILL NEED**
>
> Fabric
> Interlining
> Lining
> Fabric-covered weights, one for each corner and seam
> Sewing kit

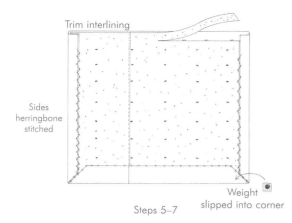

Trim interlining

Sides herringbone stitched

Weight slipped into corner

Steps 5–7

7 Measure the finished length up from the hem. Mark the top line with a row of pins. Transfer these to the right side of the fabric. Trim the interlining to this line.

8 Starting at the leading edge, lay the seamed and hemmed lining, right side uppermost, onto the curtain 4cm (1½in) up from the hem.

9 Fold back the lining and interlock to the interlining every quarter width, half width, on the seams and at 15cm (6in) in from the side edges. Stop interlocking 25cm (10in) from the top of the curtain.

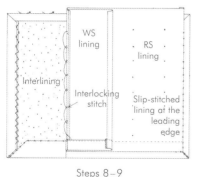

WS lining

RS lining

Interlining

Interlocking stitch

Slip-stitched lining at the leading edge

Steps 8–9

10 Trim the lining level with the side edges of the curtain and fold the raw edge under to within 4cm (1½in) of the edge and slip-stitch. At the hem, continue to slip-stitch around the corner for 5cm (2in).

11 At the hem, sew chains between the lining and the fabric (see page 95), every half width across the curtain.

12 Follow the instructions for your chosen heading (see pages 102, 108–11)

MITRED CURTAIN CORNERS

A mitre distributes the fabric evenly and should be used on the hems of all curtains, especially interlined ones.

1 Mark the corner of the mitre with a pin; this is where both the hemline and the side fold line of the curtain meet.

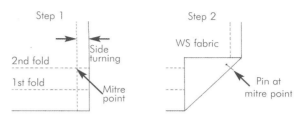

Step 1

Side turning

2nd fold

1st fold

Mitre point

Step 2

WS fabric

Pin at mitre point

2 Turn up the corner of the fabric at an angle of 45° so that the fold runs through the mitre point. Check that the raw edge of the fabric at the top of the fold lies at 90° to the side of the curtain.

3 Turn up the first and second hem folds and pin.

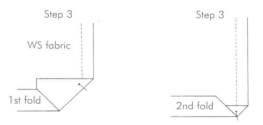

Step 3

WS fabric

1st fold

Step 3

2nd fold

4 Cover a lead weight with lining fabric and sew into the corner.

5 Fold in the side turning allowance to complete the mitre. There will be excess fabric in the corner, so tuck it inside with a pin to make a clean point. Check the corner with a set square. Slip-stitch into place.

Steps 4–5

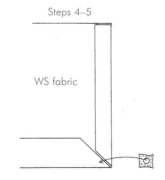

WS fabric

Making bordered curtains

Borders need to be sewn on to the main fabric before you start your curtain. To avoid puckered seams, make sure your border fabric's weight is compatible with that of the main fabric.

Decide on which borders you want – top, bottom, leading edges, or a combination, then decide on their width.

Professional tip

When you have a border on both the leading edge and the hem, you could mitre the corner for a professional finish.

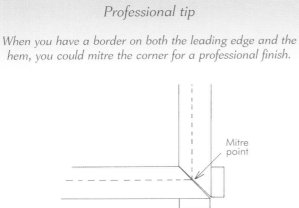

Mitre
point

ESTIMATING AND CUTTING BORDER FABRIC

When estimating and cutting fabric for your top border, allow the width of the border plus a 2cm (³⁄₄in) seam allowance and a 6cm (2¹⁄₄in) side turning allowance. If your contrast fabric is the same width as your curtain fabric, allow the same number of border widths as curtain widths.

For bottom borders allow the width of the border, plus a 2cm (³⁄₄in) seam allowance and a 24cm (9¹⁄₂in) hem allowance. Again, allow the same number of border widths as your curtain.

For leading edge borders, allow the width of the border plus a 2cm (³⁄₄in) seam allowance and a 6cm (2¹⁄₄in) side turning allowance. The cut length of the border should be the same as your curtain cut length. Leading edge borders should be made from one single length of fabric to avoid unsightly seams across the border.

SEAMING CONTRAST BORDERS ONTO A CURTAIN

1 Cut out and seam up your curtain fabric widths.

2 Seam the border strips onto the curtain in the correct order: top and bottom edges and then the leading edge last. For tops and hems, seam the border strips together. When seaming top or bottom borders to your curtain, match the seams to your main fabric seams.

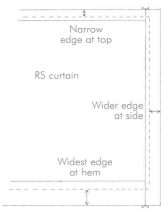

Narrow
edge at top

RS curtain

Wider edge
at side

Widest edge
at hem

3 Trim seam allowance and press open.

4 Continue to make up the curtain following your chosen method.

YOU WILL NEED

Main fabric for curtains
Contrast fabric for borders
Sewing kit

Trimming curtains

Fringes and braids are a finishing touch for leading edges of curtains.

Traditionally fringes and braids were sewn on the leading edge to protect curtain fabric as well as for decoration.

Fringes give a light look to the leading edge and can be hand-sewn or machined. Bead fringes work particularly well on sheers where they are caught by the light.

Braids give a clean and strong definition to a curtain edge, especially when you choose a strong contrasting colour. Flat braids look striking when positioned in from the leading edge. Braids come in a variety of widths.

INSETTING TRIMMINGS INTO LEADING EDGES

Any inset trimmings need to be seamed into the leading edge before making the curtain.

1 Cut out your curtain fabric widths.

2 With right side uppermost, fold back 8cm (3¼in) at the leading edge and iron all the way down.

3 Turn the fold back and place the flange of your trimming inside the creased fold. Fold the fabric back over and machine as close to the edge of the trim as possible.

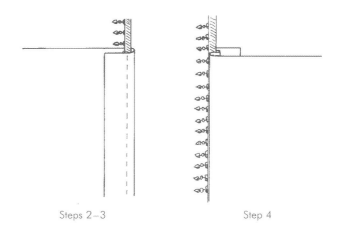

Steps 2–3   Step 4

4 Fold back the fabric to reveal the trimming. Continue to make the curtain following your chosen method.

ONSETTING FRINGES OR BRAIDS AT LEADING EDGES

Onset fringes or braids can either be hand-sewn or machined onto the leading edges of curtains.

If they are hand-sewn they can be added after the curtain is made up. When hand-sewing flat braid take small stitches to avoid the braid gaping at the sides.

Machined trimmings need to be machined in place before the curtain is made up.

Attaching gather heading tape

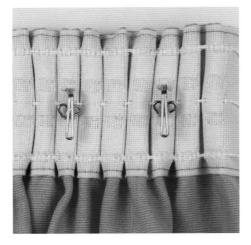

Using gather heading tape is the standard way to head your curtains. It is a woven tape with integral pockets for curtain hooks and is pulled up by a series of cords to form gathers. Tapes are sold in inch depths rather than centimetres.

There is a wide range of gather heading tape available from 1 to 6 inches deep. The most popular depths are 3 inches or 1 inch. The wider gather heading tape gives more structured gathers. One-inch tape looks softer and more informal and looks better when set down from the top of the curtain. Transluscent tape is also available for sheer curtains.

The quality of tapes varies widely. The less expensive tapes have corded pockets for inserting the hooks and the more expensive tapes have stronger woven pockets.

Some tapes are multi-pocket which gives you several hook positions. This flexibility means you can adjust the length of your curtains more easily. Hooks are available in nylon, plastic, brass or chrome finishes.

Smocked and pleated heading tapes are also available. Most tapes require 2 to 2½ times fullness.

ATTACHING MACHINE TAPES

1   Turn over the raw edge at the top of the curtain to the wrong side and pin. Trim the raw edge if necessary.

2   Pull 10cm (4in) of draw cords out at one end of the tape and tie in a secure knot.

3   Pin the tape to the curtain 3mm (⅛in) down from the top and tuck under the raw edges of the tape and the knot you have just made. Double-check that the pockets for the hooks are correctly placed (see page 91).

4   Machine up the side of the tape and along the top. Stop machining 15cm (6in) from the edge of the curtain; keep the work in the machine.

5   Cut the tape, leaving a 10cm (4in) turning allowance. Pull the drawcords out at the outside edge and tie in a secure knot. Trim any excess cord and tuck the raw edge of the tape under, enclosing the cords so that they will not pull loose.

6   Machine to the end, down the side and along the bottom so that the tape is secure.

7   At the outside edge pull up the draw cords evenly to the finished width. Tie them into a bow or wrap round a cord tidy. Remember to pull up a left-hand and right-hand curtain.

8   Insert hooks into the tape pockets every 10 to 15cm (4–6in).

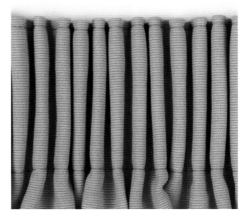

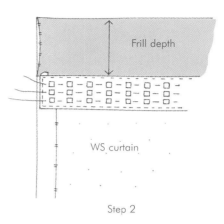

Frill depth

WS curtain

Step 2

FLOP-OVER FRILL HEADING

1 Decide on the depth of your flop-over frill, usually between 10 and 20cm (4–8in).

2 Allow double the depth of your flop-over frill, plus a 4cm (1½in) seam allowance. Cut the same number of widths as your main curtain fabric and seam together. Place right sides of the heading panel and the main curtain together and machine-sew. Press the seam allowance open.

3 Make up the curtain following your chosen method.

4 To finish the heading, fold back the flop-over frill to the required depth.

5 Place the gather heading tape on the back of the curtain over the raw edges, pin and machine in place. At the top of the tape, machine very closely to the edge so that the gather heading tape does not show at the front of the curtain heading.

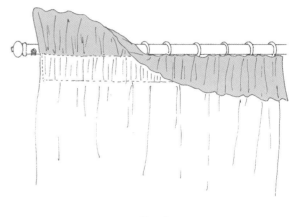

Step 5

Professional tip

To avoid unsightly cords hanging at the outside edge of your curtains, pull the cords half a width in from the outside edge. Secure the cords with a knot or a cord tidy.

Making clip-headed curtains

Double-pleated heading clipped into place.

Clips are suitable for lightweight unlined or lined curtains.

There is a wide range of clips available. Most clips will hold the curtain fabric at front and back, so are used on flat panels of fabric. These flat curtains are economical on fabric as they can use less than 1½ times fullness.

Some clips, like the ones in the picture above, grip the curtain fabric sideways, so use them for holding pleats in place: 1–1½ times fullness will be required for these clips.

Always read the clip maufacturer's instructions.

CLIP HEADINGS AND FLAT PANELS

1   Choose clips suitable for holding flat panels of fabric.

2   Neaten the raw edges at the top of your curtain.

2a For an unlined curtain, fold the top edge over twice and machine-stitch or hand-sew in place.

2b For a lined curtain, fold in the lining and fabric at the top edge and slip-stitch together.

3   Space your clips every 10 to 15cm (4–6in) apart.

CLIP HEADINGS AND PLEATED PANELS

1   Choose clips suitable for holding pleated panels of fabric.

2   Follow either step **2a** or **2b** above.

3   Form your pleats evenly across the fabric and clip in place.

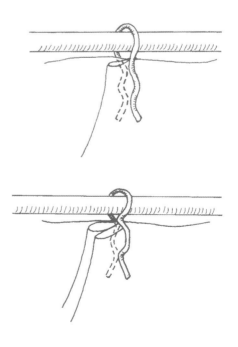

Making tab-headed curtains

Ready-made leather tabs, secured with a metal rivet, hold box pleats in place.

You can either buy ready-made tabs, or make them yourself out of the curtain fabric and sew them onto the top of your curtain.

Follow the manufacturer's instructions for attaching ready-made tabs.

For fabric tabs, follow the make-up instructions given. When attaching fabric tabs to a flat panel, you will need 1½ times fullness or less.

Allow extra face fabric to make the tabs.

When hanging curtains, to obtain the best effect, the top of the curtain (not the top of the tabs) should cover the top of the window frame or architrave.

Ready-made leather tabs with metal rivets.

ATTACHING FABRIC TABS TO A FLAT CURTAIN PANEL

Tabs are generally 4cm (1½in) wide and should be long enough to go around the pole with ease.

1   Decide on the width of your tab and the approximate space you would like between them.

2   Decide on the number of tabs required, remembering that the edges of your curtain must start and end with a tab. Space the tabs approximately 10 to 15cm (4–6in) apart.

3   The cut width of your tab is twice the width plus two 2cm (¾in) seam allowances.

4   For the cut length of your tab, measure the diameter of your pole. The cut length of your tab will be 4 x the diameter, plus two 2cm (¾in) seam allowances.

5   Cut out the required number of tabs.

6   Fold each tab in half lengthways, right sides together, and machine along the long edge, taking a 2cm (¾in) seam allowance. Press the seams open. Turn the tabs right side out and, with the seams down the centre back, press again.

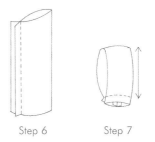

Step 6   Step 7

7   Fold the tabs in half, with the seams to the inside.

8   At the top of the curtain, fold in the face fabric and lining.

9   Starting and ending with a tab, insert the tabs to a depth of 2cm (¾in) between the fabric and lining and pin in place. Space the tabs evenly across the top of the curtain panel. Machine-stitch along the top of the curtain to secure the tabs. Remove pins and press.

Making eyelet-tape curtains

Eyelet tape usually has plastic tabs fitted to the back to hold the tape into two possible fold depths. The eyelets are usually 38mm (1½ in) in diameter.

When sewing the tape to the top of your curtains, ensure that you have an even number of eyelets and that the eyelet plastic tabs will pair up to form the folds. It may be necessary to trim the outside edge of your curtain to fit the required amount of eyelet tape.

EYELET HEADING TAPE INSTRUCTIONS

1 Place your tape on your fabric and check that you will have an even number of eyelets and that the plastic tabs will pair up. Make your curtain to this width.

2 Cut your tape to size ensuring that you cut the tape in the middle of a pair of tabbed eyelets.

3 Machine the tape onto the back of the curtain along the top, bottom and down each side.

4 With a small pair of sharp scissors, carefully cut away the fabric inside the tape eyelets leaving approximately 3mm (⅛in) of fabric around the edge of the circle.

5 On the right side of the curtain, click the eyelet ring onto the tape ring.

6 Hook the plastic tabs together at the back of the tape.

Professional tip

Place your eyelet tape on your curtain before you sew up your side turnings. This way you can ensure you do not position an eyelet over a fabric seam or have a seam on the front of a fold.

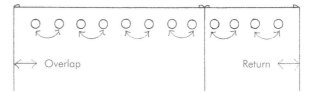

Overlap   Return

Making pressed eyelet curtains

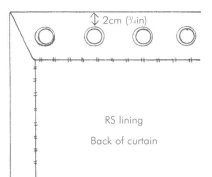

↕ 2cm (¾in)

RS lining

Back of curtain

To make pressed eyelet curtain headings, you either need a hand tool with a mallet or hammer, or an eyelet press.

If you don't have these tools, then you can send your curtains away to a specialist eyeleting company.

Individual curtain eyelets generally come in three sizes - 25mm (1in), 40mm (1½in) and 66mm (2½in), although other sizes are available. Eyelets come in a range of metallic finishes.

Pressed eyelet headings require a top turning allowance of 15cm (6in). This ensures the eyelet hole does not cut through the heading stitching.

USING AN EYELET-SETTING HAND TOOL

1   Heading buckram can be inserted in the heading if you wish. Fold in the top of the curtain 15cm (6in). Fold in the raw edge of the lining and slip-stitch to neaten.

2   Decide where you want the eyelet rings to be. The top of the outer rim of the eyelets should be set down 2cm (¾in) from the top of the curtain. Eyelets should be placed approximately 12 to 20cm (5–8in) apart. The outer rim of the first and last eyelet should be set in from the edge by half the width of the space between the eyelets. Increase the return measurement if necessary. Make sure you have an even number of eyelets. Mark the centres of the eyelets with pins. Ensure any seams fall between paired eyelets.

3   Using sharp scissors, cut out the fabric just slightly less than the circumference of the eyelet. You could use a cardboard template of the inside of the ring to ensure that all your holes are equal in size.

4   Place the curtain, wrong side uppermost, on a firm surface that will take the weight of your hammering.

5   Position the front ring behind the hole and smooth the fabric over the rim.

6   Place the back ring over the lining and the rim of the front ring. Position the hand setting tool over the eyelet and hammer closed with the mallet. It may take as many as 20 hits to close the eyelets properly.

7   Repeat steps **5–6** for the remaining eyelets.

USING AN EYELET PRESS

Follow steps **1–2** above. Use the eyelet press to cut your hole. Place the back eyelet on the press. With fabric right side uppermost, align the cut hole with the back eyelet and cover with the front eyelet. Lower the lever to close the eyelet. Repeat for your remaining eyelets.

Making pleat-headed curtains

Pleat-headed curtains are stiffened with heading buckram which allows the fabric to fall in neat, structured folds. Heading buckram is a stiffened white cotton fabric and comes in widths of 10 to 15cm (4–6in). It can be treated with a heat-soluble glue on one or both sides to make it 'fusible'.

Single-sided fusible heading buckram is placed at the top of the curtain between the face fabric and the lining. With the fusible side facing the lining, it is ironed to hold it in position. Double-sided fusible heading buckram is used on interlined curtains and is sandwiched between the interlining and lining and then ironed in position. Non-fusible buckram can be used on all curtains and gives a softer look.

The curtain heading is folded and sewn to form simple pleats which are supported by the stiffened buckram. These pleats are folded again and hand-sewn to form different styles of pleat.

Pin hooks are inserted into the lining and buckram at the back of the curtain.

CALCULATING THE SIZE OF PLEATS, AND SPACES

To start, you will need the required finished width and the actual flat width of your curtain.

Note down the finished width of the curtain (see page 91).

To establish the flat width of the curtain, measure across the top and note the measurement down.

Now you can work out the number of pleats and spaces for your curtain. As a standard rule, allow four pleats per fabric width.

A curtain will always have one less space than it has pleats, plus an overlap at the leading edge and a return at the outside edge.

Individual pleats should be between 15 and 20cm (6–8in), with the spaces between them 10 and 15cm (4–6in) wide. Overlaps are usually 7cm (2¾in) and returns are usually 10cm (4in).

In simple terms, all the space measurements, plus overlap and return add up to the finished width of the heading. The remainder of the flat measurement is the fullness, which is then divided evenly into the pleats.

Rolls of heading buckram

PLEATING PLAIN FABRIC

1   Subtract the finished width of the curtain heading from the flat width. This gives the fullness to be pleated.

2   Divide the fullness by the number of pleats to find their size (allow four pleats per fabric width).

    If the pleat size is too small, i.e. less than 15cm (6in), re-calculate, dividing by one less pleat. If it is too big, i.e. over 20cm (8in), re-calculate, dividing by one more pleat.

3   To find the size of the spaces, take the finished width of the heading and subtract the overlap and return measurements. Divide this figure by the number of spaces (one less than the number of pleats).

4   Double-check your calculations.

PLEATING PATTERNED FABRIC

For patterned fabrics it is better to work out your pleats and spaces on your seamed-up fabric before you have turned in the side edges. This means that you can start the leading edge of your curtain at the right part of the pattern.

Establish the required finished width and the actual flat width of the curtain heading, plus the overlap and return measurements, as for pleating plain fabric.

The calculation will be different from plain fabric as the number of pleats is dictated by the pattern. Decide on which part of the pattern to position the pleat. This is the part of the fabric design you will see when the curtains are stacked back and the pleats compressed.

1   To establish the number of pleats, place a pin at the centre of each motif or stripe across the flat curtain width. Note down the number of pins. This will be the number of pleats for your curtain.

2   Remember that you will have one less space than pleats, so note this figure down also.

3   To find the size of each space, begin by measuring the horizontal pattern repeat, i.e. the distance between the pins, and how many times it recurs. Note these figures down.

    Now take the finished width of the curtain heading, subtract the overlap and return measurements and divide this figure by the number of spaces between the pleats.

4   To determine the pleat size, subtract the space measurement from the horizontal pattern repeat.

5   Mark the pleat and space measurements with pins along the top of each panel.

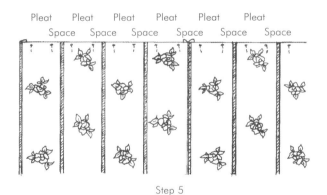

Step 5

The depth of the buckram depends on the choice of the heading.

The standard pre-cut sizes are 10cm (4in), 12.5cm (5in) and 15cm (6in).

For goblets, inverted pleats, pin-hook pleats and Tête de Versailles use 10cm (4in) buckram.

For French headings and box-pleat headings use 12.5cm (5in) buckram.

Use 15cm (6in) buckram for very long curtains over 3 metres (10ft).

Steps **1–4** actually form a Tête de Versailles pleat. French, goblet, and box pleats all start with the same four steps, but are each then finished differently to create their specific styles.

INSERTING BUCKRAM

1   At the top of the heading, fold over the turning allowance. On the right side, mark with pins the pleats and space measurements.

2   With a row of interlocking stitches, sew the buckram onto the interlining across the lower edge. If you are only using lining, sew the buckram as invisibly as possible to the fabric to hold it in place. If using fusible buckram, iron it in place as well.

3   Fold in the raw edge of the lining and slip-stitch to the fabric.

4   Pin the pleats together, ensuring that the top edges are level, and sew down to the bottom of the buckram.

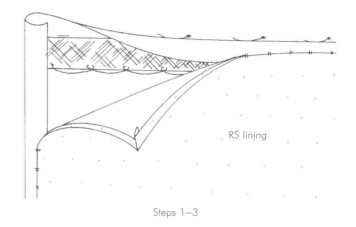

RS lining

Steps 1–3

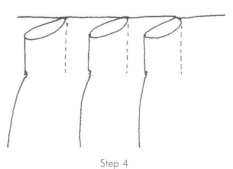

Step 4

Professional tip

Buckram, plus curtain fabric and lining, may be too thick to go through a domestic sewing machine. If this is the case then hand-sew down the sides of the pleats. If the curtain is interlined as well, then you will definitely have to hand-sew the pleats in place.

TÊTE DE VERSAILLES

Follow steps **1–4** for inserting buckram to form single pleats.

INVERTED PLEATS

Follow steps **1–4** for inserting buckram, but at step **1**, make the pleats on the wrong side of the fabric.

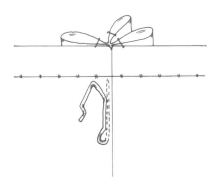

FRENCH PLEATS

Follow steps **1–4.** To divide the pleat into three folds, hold the fold, and push it down gently to form three equal sections. Bring them together at the base and hand-sew through the bottom of the pleat, just beneath the buckram. Sew the side pleats to the top edge of the curtain, either side of the seam. Sew the top edges of the middle pleat together. If your pleats are small, you can divide them into two sections rather than three.

GOBLET PLEATS

After steps **1–4**, fold the bottom of the pleat as for a French pleat and sew through the base to secure. Shape into a tube and hand-sew the goblet either side of the seam to the top edge. To retain the shape stuff the goblet with wadding.

BOX PLEATS

Follow steps **1–4** then flatten out the pleat and hand-sew the outside edges at the top. Secure the base of the pleat at the outside edges with very small stab stitches taken through to the back of the curtain.

ADDING HOOKS TO PLEATED HEADINGS

Stab pin hooks into the buckram at the side of each pleat, at a level which will give you the required hook position (see page 91). Take care not to stab through the stitch line as it will weaken the stitching.

If the track or pole has overlap arms, position the hooks at the leading edge of the curtain to correspond with them.

PIN-HOOK HEADINGS

Follow steps **1–3** to insert the buckram. Insert your pin hooks in the correct positions for your pleats and spaces. Catch the fabrics together at the top and bottom of the hooks with small stab stitches which go through to the front of the fabric. Place two hooks in the eye of the glider or pole ring.

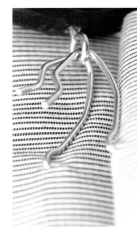

Making fabric-covered laths

The track is fitted to the underside of a 10cm (4in) wide x 2.5cm (1in) piece of planed timber. This piece of wood forms your pelmet board.

The track is concealed by a thin 3mm (⅛in) hardboard fascia which is stapled or tacked to the front edge. The fascia is cut to a depth that covers the track but still allows the hooks and overlap arms free movement.

The pelmet board and fascia are then covered by fabric before the track is screwed in place.

1 Cut your pelmet board and fascia to the width of the track. The fascia depth needs to be cut to the depth of the timber plus the depth of the track profile, excluding gliders. Staple or tack the fascia to the pelmet board.

2 Staple fabric to your board and fascia.

3 Top-fix the track to the pelmet board directly behind the fascia.

4 Fit vine eyes at each end of the pelmet board for the curtain return.

5 Fit brackets to the wall. If your pelmet board is long, you may need a centre bracket. Screw your fabric-covered lath in place.

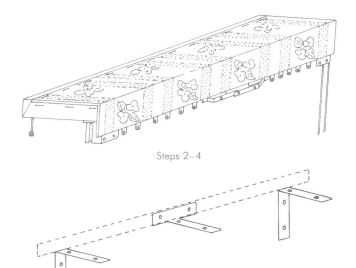

Steps 2–4

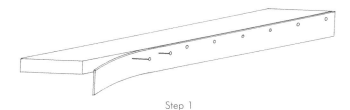

Step 1

Step 5

YOU WILL NEED

10 x 2.5cm (4 x 1in) planed
timber, x length of your track
3mm (⅛) hardboard,
approximately 4.5cm (1¾in) wide.
2 x angle brackets
1 x T bracket
2 x vine eyes (long screw eyes)
Tool kit for fixing

HANGING CURTAINS

Set the ladder so that you have the least amount of stretching to do.

Remove any spare gliders or rings from tracks and poles.

Use silicon spray to make the gliders or rings run smoothly. Spray this onto a duster and run it along the top of the pole or the inside groove of the track.

With a multi-layered treatment, start by hanging the layer nearest to the window glass and work outwards.

Put the curtains over one shoulder to take the weight. Start hanging the curtains from the centre of the track. Never start by hooking them onto the overlap arm as the weight will bend it or, worse still, snap it off completely.

If you wish to return your curtains then the outside edges of the curtains should be hooked onto a screw eye so that the curtains are returned to the wall.

Once hung, draw and close the curtains and make sure that they meet correctly in the middle.

CURTAIN CARE

Curtains should be vacuumed regularly to keep them free of dust.

Curtains can be dry-cleaned at a specialist dry-cleaners. Some unlined and ready-made curtains can be washed in the washing machine, so follow the given instructions carefully to ensure the best result.

Tracks and poles should be cleaned on occasion, but wax polishes should be avoided as they may leave a sticky residue which attracts dust over time.

DRESSING CURTAINS

When curtains are first hung they should be dressed to encourage them to fall into even rounded folds. Interlined curtains respond especially well to this process.

To dress the curtains, start by drawing them back into their stack-back position. Then, starting from the outside edge, working from the top downwards, run your hands firmly down the length of each pleat or fold.

For goblet or French pleats hung from a pole, or a track where the top of the curtain hangs below it, push the spaces between the hooks to the back. Where curtains are hung from a lath with a fascia or where the heading hangs in front of the track, pull the spaces between the hooks forward.

TO BANDAGE CURTAINS

Tie three strips of waste lining or fabric to make bandages around each curtain. They should hold the folds in position but they should not be so tight that they leave indentation marks.

Leave for two or three days. Remove the ties and draw the curtains. They should then hang in set folds.

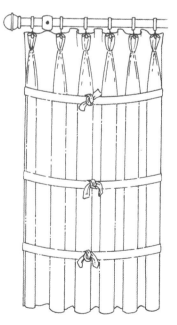

Cushions

Cushions

Cushion essentials and make-up

"Cushions add colour and comfort"

Cushions

Cushions are the final flourish in a room, and are often the last thing to be decided in the scheme.

Adding warmth and comfort to sofas and softening the hard edges of furnishings, cushions suit every style, whether modern or traditional.

They are an opportunity to combine a variety of fabrics and textures, and are a way of enjoying expensive or luxurious fabrics in small quantities.

Although there is a range of cushion shapes available (bolsters, round and even heart-shaped), square cushions are the most popular. They combine well with rectangular cushions on seating and beds.

Cushion pads can be filled with feathers or synthetic fillings. Whatever filling you choose, ensure your cushions are full and plump to gain the most luxurious look.

Piping and trimmings are the finishing touches for a cushion. Cushions allow you to include small quantities of beautiful trimmings in your room.

Left and right   A variety of co-ordinating cushions have been carefully chosen and placed to look inviting.

Use cushions to link different
elements of a scheme in a room.

Consider the overall scheme and use cushion
covers to repeat fabrics, designs or colours used
elsewhere in the room. Cushions can also be used
to add splashes of colour on neutral furniture.

Cushions usually look better when placed squarely
rather than on their tips. If a cushion cover is
made from a striped or strong geometric design,
then, as a general rule, the pattern should run
vertically rather than horizontally.

Left   The front cushion co-ordinates with and the
back cushion repeats the curtain fabric.

Right   The cushion fabric echoes the wallpaper
design and looks striking and contemporary.

"Cushions look best when placed squarely on the seat"

Bring soft luxury to your bedroom with cushions.

Pile your bed high with a variety of cushion sizes and use pretty fabrics in complementary colours.

Cushions on beds work well with co-ordinating throws and simple, plain bedlinen.

Just as on sofas and chairs, cushions need to be carefully placed to look good. Also, to keep your cushions looking smart, ensure you plump them up regularly.

Left and right Beds piled high with cushions which echo and co-ordinate with the curtain fabrics and colour scheme.

"Cushions can make seats look more inviting"

Cushions are a good first sewing project.

Using small amounts of fabric, cushions are rewarding to make.

Cushions can be made fairly simply and easily. They are also an opportunity to explore your creative side and bring individual touches to your home.

Using fabrics that you love, you can personalise your rooms with cushions.

Whether you want plain, tied, Oxford, panelled, bordered or piped cushions, you can follow our step-by-step instructions to make beautiful cushions.

Left and far left Cushions add a soft touch to garden furniture.

Cushion essentials and make-up

This section includes general information about cushions and cutting covers; making basic cushion covers; inserting zips; and making piped, envelope, Oxford, panelled, tied, contrast-banded and trimmed cushion covers.

The make-up techniques described here are used in our workroom. Experienced sewers may wish to adapt the methods to suit the way they work.

CUSHION FILLINGS

Cushion pads can be filled with either feathers or synthetic fillings. Feathers are the best filling for cushions because they do not go lumpy or flat.

The least expensive feather filling is curled chicken feathers. The feathers have been curled to give them volume. Over time the curling will drop out and flatten. Chicken feather cushion pads may have an odour.

Duck feather pads have better recovery than chicken feather pads. They are naturally curly and are usually combined with 20% down. For the most luxurious filling, choose goose and duck down, but this is the most expensive option.

Feather cushion pads are covered in a waxed cambric. The waxed side is used on the inside of the cover to prevent the feathers from working their way out.

Hollow polyester fibre is the most popular synthetic cushion filling. It has good recovery, but doesn't have the softness of duck feather. It is also suitable for people with allergies. Hollowfibre cushions will flatten over time, so make sure that they are plump at the beginning to get the best use out of them.

CUSHION PADS

Square, round and bolster cushion pads are readily available in a range of sizes. Specialist manufacturers can make bespoke pads from paper templates.

COVER SIZES AND CUTTING NOTES

The cover should be smaller than the cushion pad to ensure a snug fit. For pads from 30 to 40cm (12–16in), make the finished cover size 2.5cm (1in) smaller than the pad. For pads from 46 to 61cm (18–24in), make the cover 5cm (2in) smaller. For pad sizes outside these ranges, it is best to make a mock cover from lining first to establish the finished cover size that fits best.

Once you have decided on the finished cover size you want, add a 2cm (³/₄in) seam allowance all round. Then make a paper pattern the cut size of the cover.

When cutting out cushion covers in patterned fabrics centralise the pattern on both the front and back cover. Although this can waste a lot of fabric, the pattern is the key focal point and it is vital to do this. The front and back cover patterns need not be the same.

ZIP FASTENINGS

Zip inserted next to the piping, viewed from the back of the cushion.

Zips are a practical and neat solution for closing cushion covers. Cushion covers can easily be removed for cleaning if they are made with a zip opening. Take care, when removing or inserting the cushion pad into the cover, not to break the stitching around the corner of the cover.

CHOOSING ZIPS

Use a No.3 dressmaking zip which matches the cushion fabric. If you can't get an exact match always choose a slightly darker zip colour as it will be less obvious than a paler one. For patterned fabrics choose zips which match, or are slightly darker than, the background colour.

Choose a zip length that is 5cm (2in) less than the lower edge of finished cushion cover. If a zip is too long it can be easily cut down to size. Measure the required length from the top of the zip. With a hand-sewing needle and double thread, over-sew a bar of stitches to prevent the zipper tab from detatching from the teeth. Cut the zip 1.5cm ($^5/_8$in) below your bar of stitches.

INSERTING A ZIP AND SEAMING THE COVER TOGETHER

If you haven't inserted a zip before, take your time and read the instructions carefully. For a first project, start with simple plain cushions.

1   Change the foot on your sewing machine to the zip foot.

2   With the right side of the front cover uppermost, place the zip face down and align the centre of the zip with your 2cm ($^3/_4$in) seam allowance on the bottom edge of the fabric. Carefully machine 2cm ($^3/_4$in) down the outer edge only, as close to the teeth as possible but not beyond them.

RS fabric

Step 2

3   Before you sew the other side of the zip, lay the front cover on top of the back cover, right sides together. Starting at one end of the zip, machine around the three edges, taking a 2cm ($^3/_4$in) seam allowance and stopping at the other end of the zip. Take care not to catch the top and bottom zip flaps into the stitching.

WS fabric

Step 3

4   To attach the zip to the back cover, carefully machine the zip to the back cover lower edge, taking a 2cm ($^3/_4$in) seam allowance, as close to the teeth as possible. Stop within 5cm (2in) of the top of the zip leaving the needle in the work.

WS fabric

Step 4

Lift the machine foot and open the zip below it. Continue to sew the zip to the top, again ensuring that you take a 2cm ($^3/_4$in) seam allowance.

Making a plain cushion cover

Plain cushions are the simplest of cushions and work well in all styles and types of rooms.

The fronts and backs of plain cushions can be made from different fabrics, allowing you to turn your cushion around to show a different material. This adds variety to your scheme and also means you get two cushion looks in one.

If you are a complete novice sewer you may find it easier to hand-sew the cushion cover opening closed, rather than inserting a zip.

1 Cut out a paper pattern the size of the finished cover, plus a 2cm (¾in) seam allowance. (See cover sizes and cutting allowance, page 124.)

2 Place the paper pattern on the fabric and cut out the front and back cover. If using a patterned fabric, centre the cover over a part of the design that you want to feature.

Step 2

3 Neaten the edges of the front and back covers by sewing around each side using a zigzag stitch. This will prevent the fabric from fraying.

4 Insert zip (see page 125).

5 Machine all round, taking a 2cm (¾in) seam allowance. Trim the seam allowance at the corners and turn the cover through to the right side, easing out the corners. Press. Insert the cushion pad and plump into shape.

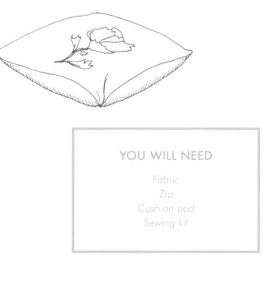

YOU WILL NEED

Fabric
Zip
Cushion pad
Sewing kit

Making a piped cushion cover

Piping defines the edge of a cushion and looks particularly good in a contrast colour.

MAKING A PIPED COVER

Follow steps **1–2** as for a plain cushion cover, see page opposite.

1 Make your piping (see page 135).

2 Starting in the middle of the bottom edge of the cushion, place the piping on the right side of the front cover with the raw edges level.

3 Machine the piping in place. To allow the piping to pivot at the corners, leave the needle in the fabric at the corner point and lift the machine foot. Snip the piping seam allowance to just within the stitch line. Turn the cover and fold the piping around the corner. Lower the foot and continue machining the piping around the cover.

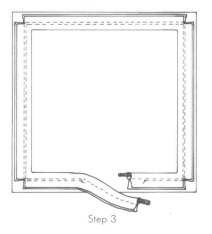

Step 3

4 To join the piping, cut the piping cord so that it butts together. On one side, trim the fabric up to the cord and on the other side leave 4cm (1½in) of fabric. Fold in the raw edge, overlap by 2cm (¾in) and machine across.

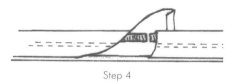

Step 4

5 Now insert the zip and seam the cover together (see page 125). At step **3** of inserting the zip, lay the front cover on top of the back cover, right sides together, and machine as close as possible to the line of stitching used to attach the piping.

6 Trim the seam allowance at the corners and turn the cover through to the right side, easing out the corners. Press. Insert the cushion pad and plump into shape.

YOU WILL NEED

Cushion fabric
Piping fabric
Piping cord
Zip
Cushion pad
Sewing kit

Making an envelope cushion cover

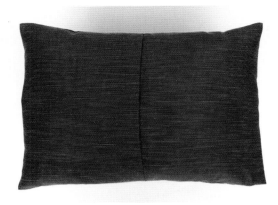

An envelope opening is an alternative to a zip. Envelope openings can be used at the back, or at the front of the cushion if they are embellished with buttons or ties.

The envelope overlap is usually 10cm (4in).

For retangular cushions the opening can either be horizontal or vertical.

1 Cut out a paper pattern the size of the finished cover, plus 2cm (³⁄₄in) seam allowances all round. See cover sizes and cutting notes (see page 124).

2 Place the paper pattern on the fabric and cut out the front cover. If using a patterned fabric, centre the cover over a part of the design that you want to feature.

3 The back cover will be made from two pieces of fabric. To make a paper back cover pattern for the upper section, fold the front cover paper pattern in half and add a further 4cm (1¹⁄₂in) turning allowance to the centre side and cut out. Use the pattern to cut out your fabric.

Take the back cover paper pattern and add an extra 15cm (6in) to make the lower section pattern (this includes your turning allowances) and cut out. Use the patterns to cut out your fabric. If using a patterned fabric, match the pattern as far as possible on the two back cover sections.

4 Neaten the edges of all the panels by sewing around each side using a zigzag stitch. This will prevent the fabric from fraying.

5 Working on the back cover upper section, fold over 2cm (³⁄₄in) turning allowance twice along the envelope edge and machine. Repeat for the lower section.

6 Place the front cover onto the table right side uppermost. Lay the upper section of the back cover face down onto the front cover and then lay the lower section on top of this. Pin in place.

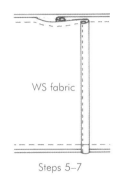

WS fabric

Steps 5–7

7 Machine all round, taking a 2cm (³⁄₄in) seam allowance. Trim the seam allowance at the corners and turn the cover through to the right side, easing out the corners. Press. Insert the cushion pad and plump into shape.

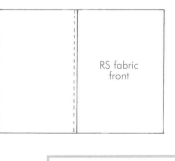

RS fabric
front

YOU WILL NEED

Fabric
Paper for pattern
Cushion pad
Sewing kit

Making an Oxford envelope cushion cover

An Oxford cushion has a flat flange, or edge, around the sides of the cushion.

The flange is a flat fabric border created by cutting the cushion cover extra large and stitching a line inset from the edge.

1 Decide on the size of the flat flange for your cushion; flanges are usually between 2.5 and 5cm (1–2in).

2 Cut out a paper pattern the size of the finished cover, adding a 2cm (³⁄₄in) seam allowance and the size of your flange all around (see page 124 for cover sizes and cutting notes).

3 Follow steps **2–6** as given for making an envelope cushion cover.

4 Machine all round, taking a 2cm (³⁄₄in) seam allowance. Trim the seam allowance at the corners, turn the cover through to the right side and ease out the corners. Now press the cover.

5 Pin the flange size around the cover and machine-stitch to the required depth. Insert the cushion pad and plump into shape.

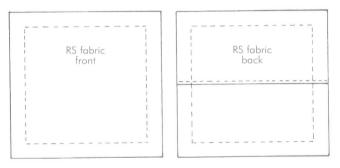

RS fabric front

RS fabric back

Step 5

Making a panelled cushion cover

Panelled cushions can echo panels and borders in curtains and blinds or draw a colour scheme together if you choose a complementing fabric.

If you're on a budget, you can still use touches of expensive and sumptuous fabrics on bordered and panelled cushions without breaking the bank.

Adding a border to a cushion can really make it stand out on your chair or sofa.

Professional tip

If you are using a lightweight, delicate fabric for your cushion cover, then you can back it with lining or a suitable fabric. It will be easier to machine and should last longer.

1 Cut out a preliminary paper pattern the size of the finished cover, without seam allowances (see cover sizes and cutting notes on page 124). Draw in the panel lines and cut through to give a paper pattern for each panel.

2 Lay the centre pattern on a new piece of paper. Draw round the pattern, adding a 2cm (¾in) seam allowance all around, and cut out. This will give you the paper pattern for your fabric. Repeat for one of the side panels.

3 Using the paper panels, cut out two centre panels and four side panels. If using a patterned fabric, centre the cover over a part of the design that you want to feature.

4 Neaten the edges of all the panels by sewing around each side using a zigzag stitch. This will prevent the fabric from fraying.

5 Seam a side panel onto each side of a centre panel, taking a 2cm (¾in) seam allowance. Press the seams away from the lighter coloured fabric.

Steps 5–6

6 Insert the zip and seam the cover together (see page 125).

7 Trim the seam allowance at the corners and turn the cover through to the right side, easing out the corners. Press. Insert the cushion pad and plump into shape.

YOU WILL NEED

Centre panel fabric
Side panel fabric
Paper for pattern
Zip
Cushion pad
Sewing kit

Making a tied cushion cover

1　Cut out a paper pattern the size of the finished cushion cover, plus 2cm (¾in) seam allowances all round.

2　To make the front pattern, copy the back pattern and mark where you want the tied opening to be. Cut the panel along this line to create a left and right pattern for your front cover. Here we are using an off-centre opening in a rectangular cushion.

3　Cut out the back and the left and right front panels in the fabric combinations of your choice. If using a patterned fabric, centre the cover over a part of the design that you want to feature.

4　Neaten the edges of all the panels by sewing around each side using a zigzag stitch. This will prevent the fabric from fraying.

5　Cut out four ties, 4cm (1½in) wide x 30 to 40cm (12–16in) long, on the straight grain of the fabric.

Step 6

6　To make a tie, lay the fabric, wrong side uppermost, fold in and press 1cm (⅜in) on two long ends and one short end. Fold in half again lengthways and press. Machine around the end and down the length. Repeat for the remaining ties.

7　Position two ties on the opening edge of each front panel. With right side of the front cover fabric uppermost, pin the raw edge of the ties in place, level with the edge of the cover fabric. Ensure you line up your ties on the two panels.

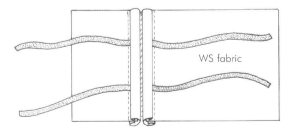

Steps 7– 9

8　Cut two strips of binding, 4cm (1½in) wide x the length of the cover opening, on the straight grain of the fabric. Take a strip of binding, wrong side uppermost, turn in 1cm (⅜in) on one long edge and press. Repeat for the second strip.

9　Take one strip of binding, wrong side uppermost and lay over the front cover and ties, aligning the raw edge with the edge of the opening. Machine the binding taking a 1cm (⅜in) seam allowance. Fold the binding round to the back. On the back, ensure the binding covers the first machine line and pin in place. On the right side, machine a row of stitching in the seam line between the main fabric and the binding. The stitches will sink into the seam and hardly show (see page 135).

10　Cut an inside front panel in the fabric colour of your choice, 15cm (6in) wide by the depth of your cut cover. Hem the two long edges, turning in 2cm (¾in) twice.

11　Place the back cover onto the table right side uppermost. Lay the front panels on top, right sides down. Then lay the inside front panel, right side down on top of the tied opening. Pin in place.

12　Machine all round the outer edge, taking a 2cm (¾in) seam allowance. Trim the seam allowance at the corners and turn the cover through to the right side, easing out the corners. Press. Insert the cushion pad and plump into shape.

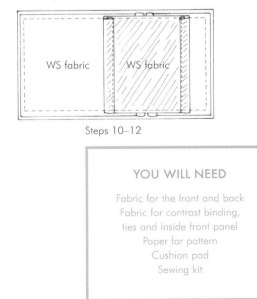

Steps 10–12

YOU WILL NEED

Fabric for the front and back
Fabric for contrast binding,
ties and inside front panel
Paper for pattern
Cushion pad
Sewing kit

Making a contrast-banded cushion cover

Contrast bands can be used to define cushion edges and frame a pattern.

A band of plain, contrasting fabric, known as a gusset, is sewn between the front and back panels.

For bands less than 5cm (2in), insert an ordinary cushion pad, remembering that the gusset enlarges the cover, so use a pad larger than the finished size of the cover. This will ensure you have a plump, finished cushion.

For 5 to 7.5cm (2–3in) bands, insert a boxed cushion pad to get the best effect.

1   Follow steps **1–3** as given for making a plain cushion cover.

2   Decide on the depth of your gusset. Measure all around the cover to find the exact length of the gusset. For the width, allow for the depth of the cushion pad gusset plus two x 2cm (¾in) seam allowances, and cut out.

If you have to cut more than one length of fabric, then seam the lengths together, but make sure that the seams will be positioned towards the bottom of your cushion.

3   Machine a zigzag stitch around all the gusset edges to neaten. Join the gusset to make a circle of fabric to fit the finished cover size.

4   Take the front cover and the seamed gusset and place, right sides together, with the seam at the bottom of your cover. Seam the gusset around the front cover, taking a 2cm (¾in) seam allowance.

Step 4

To allow the gusset to pivot at the corners, leave the needle in the fabric at the corner point and lift the foot. Snip the gusset seam allowance to just within the corner point. Turn the cover and fold the gusset around the corner. Lower the foot and continue machining along the straight edge. Repeat for all corners.

5   On the bottom edge of the gusset, insert the zip, following the steps on page 125. Then lay the back cover onto the gusset and seam together, taking a 2cm (¾in) seam allowance and taking care to align the corner points on the front and back covers.

6   Trim the seam allowance at the corners and turn the cover through to the right side, easing out the corners. Press. Insert the cushion pad and plump into shape.

Step 6

YOU WILL NEED

Cover fabric
Contrasting fabric
Zip
Cushion pad
Sewing kit

TRIMMING CUSHIONS

Fringes on cushions can enliven plain or patterned fabrics.

INSET FRINGES

To inset a fringe follow the instructions on page 127, substituting your trimming for the piping. Alternatively, sew your trimmings to the fabric when seaming together.

ONSET FRINGES

Trims and fringes can be hand-sewn onto cushion covers after they have been made up.

Close-up of a panelled cushion with bead trim inset in panel seam.

CUSHION CARE

When inserting cushion pads into covers make sure that the corners of the pad are tucked right into the corners of the cover.

To plump up a square feather cushion, hold opposite corners and bring together several times to introduce air into the cushion. Repeat the action holding the other corners. As the fabric is waxed, the only place that air can enter the cushion is at the seams.

To plump a hollowfibre cushion, hit the cushion in the centre. This will not only introduce air, but also send the fibres back out to the corners.

CLEANING CUSHIONS

Dry-cleaning or machine-washing will destroy hollowfibre fillings. However, they can be gently handwashed if necessary. The best option is to replace soiled hollowfibre cushions.

Feather cushions can be machine-washed, but not tumble-dried. They need to be air-dried slowly, but throughly. Again, replacement is often the best option.

Sewing skills

LADDER STITCH

A small, scarcely visible stitch used on mitred corners.

Knot the thread and take a short stitch through the fold of the fabric at the corner of the mitre. Take the next stitch through and into the other fold, starting opposite the previous stitch. Bring the needle out of the fold and pull the thread taut to keep the two pieces of fabric together. Repeat.

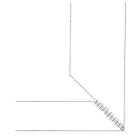
Ladder stitch

SLIP STITCH

Used to attach lining fabric.

When attaching the lining to the side of a curtain, the slip stitches can be 2cm (¾in) long. When taking the stitch through the fabric, take care not to go through to the right side.

Lining

Slip stitch

HEMMING STITCH

Can be used on hems. Hems can also be slip-stitched.

Knot the thread and take a 2cm (¾in) stitch through the fold of the hem. Take a small stitch directly above and then a long stitch back into the fold. The small stitches will be barely noticeable.

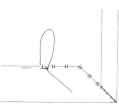
Hemming stitch

HERRINGBONE STITCH

Used for sewing the sides of interlined curtains before the lining is attached.

Worked from left to right, the needle points to the left, keeping the thread on the right-hand side of the stitching.

Interlining

Herringbone stitch

INTERLOCKING STITCH

A long and loose blanket stitch used for sewing interlining to fabrics and lining to interlining, holding the layers together while allowing some slight movement between them.

Use a continuous length of thread, no matter how long the curtain or panel. Work from the hem to the top. The stitches should be barely visible on the right side and loose enough to avoid dimples but not so loose as to be ineffective.

Long stitch

Interlining

Interlocking stitch

SPOT TACK

Two or three very small stitches oversewn on top of each other. Match the thread to the face fabric.

Knot the thread and work from the back of the fabric to the front, over-sewing each stitch.

Professional tip

Machining over pins placed at right angles is easy to do and it helps to keep all the fabric neatly in place, particularly when the fabric is slippery.

Watch out for a blunt needle. When it goes over the pin it may be slightly nicked, so it should be replaced frequently.

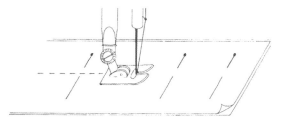

SINK STITCHING

Binding can be machine sink-stitched in place rather than slip-stitched by hand.

Make sure the binding at the back covers the machine line on the right side and pin the binding in place, with the pins placed at right angles to the seam.

On the right side, machine a row of stitching in the groove created by the seam of the main fabric and the contrast. The stitches will sink into the seam and hardly show.

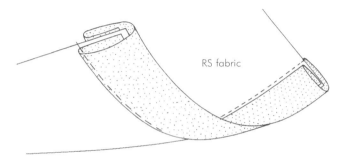

RS fabric

IRONING

Iron your curtains and blinds at every stage of the make-up process. Do not iron the side and hem edges of interlined blinds and curtains as you want them to be soft and rounded.

If you are concerned about your fabrics, linings, interlinings or trimmings shrinking, then use a steam iron on them first before making up.

A normal domestic iron is suitable for curtain and blind making. Professional steam irons reach a higher temperature than domestic irons and have a large reservoir which will provide you with steam all day.

Mobile steamers are available for removing fold lines and creases in blinds and curtains once hung.

MAKING PIPING

Piping fabric is cut at 45° to the selvedge. This is the 'true cross of the grain' and it uses the 'give' or the stretch of the fabric to let the trim lie flat. This can then be sewn around curves without puckering.

Piping is usually cut 5cm (2in) wide. Check this is sufficient for the piping cord you wish to use and cut wider strips if necessary. Thicker fabrics will need heavier piping cord and wider strips.

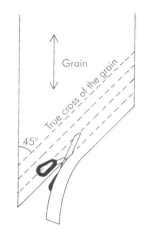

Grain

True cross of the grain

45°

1   Cut bias strips wide enough to fold over the piping cord, plus a 2cm (³⁄₄in) seam allowance.

2   If possible, cut long strips to avoid joins. If you need to join strips, then lay them right sides together at right angles and machine across the diagonal. Trim seam and press open.

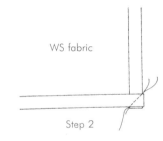

WS fabric

Step 2

3   Lay the cord in the centre of the wrong side of the strip and fold in half. Using a zip foot, machine as close as possible to the cord.

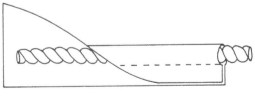

Step 3

Glossary

ACORN
Acorn-shaped toggle, made from wood or metal, used for retaining the tied ends of Roman blind cords and making them hang straight.

ARCHITRAVE
The wooden surround to a door or window.

BLACK BOLTON TWILL
A black densely-woven fabric used as an interliner for blacking out light in blinds and curtains. If the face fabric is light-coloured, use black Bolton twill in conjunction with interlining. It will make curtains or blinds heavy.

BLACKOUT LINING
A cotton or polycotton fabric that has been laminated to block out light. The laminate makes the blackout lining heavier and stiffer than standard lining fabric. Once the laminate has been pierced by a needle the stitch holes will allow light in.

BLIND CLEAT
Normally made from metal with projecting arms, used for securing blind cord. Cleats are screwed to the window frame or wall at an accessible height. Available in a range of metal finishes to suit your scheme.

BLIND CORD
A speciality braided cord, usually 1.2mm ($\frac{1}{8}$in) diameter. Stronger blind cords have a central core and so will last longer. Standard colours are white and off-white.

BLIND RINGS
12mm ($\frac{1}{2}$in) hollow brass, solid brass or plastic rings, sewn onto the back of Roman blinds to guide the cords. Transparent ones are the most discreet.

BLIND SAFETY CLIP
Small wall-fixed plastic clip designed to retain the blind cord or chain back to the wall.

BOLSTER CUSHION
Cylindrical, narrow cushion used as an arm or head rest.

BRADAWL
A pointed tool for making small holes in wood for screws.

BUMP
A soft, cotton, blanket-like fabric used as interlining. *See also* INTERLINING.

CAMBRIC
A finely woven white cotton.

CONTRAST BINDING
Strips of contrasting fabric cut on the fabric bias, sewn onto the edges of soft furnishings for a decorative effect.

CORD CONNECTOR
A two-piece housing designed to tidy cords for Roman blinds. The blind lifting cords are fed into the top half and knotted off. A single 3mm ($\frac{1}{8}$in) cord hangs from the bottom half and the two halves are screwed together.

CORD TIDY
A small, flat waisted piece of plastic around which curtain draw cords are wound.

CORD WEIGHTS
Heavy acorn-shaped metal weights which tension the curtain cords used for opening and closing the curtains. Available in a range of metal finishes. They are larger than blind acorns.

COVING
Decorative or curved moulding where the ceiling meets the wall.

CURTAIN FULLNESS
The ratio between the track or pole and the width of the ungathered curtain.

CURTAIN TRACK GLIDER
A metal or plastic runner which moves along the curtain track, with an eye into which curtain hooks are inserted.

CUSHION PADS
Ready-made pads or pillows with various soft fillings. Inserted into decorative cushion covers.

CUSHION TEMPLATE
A multi-size, transparent, flexible plastic pattern used as a guide for cutting fabric. It has punched holes at different measurements for marking through. Templates make positioning the pattern of the fabric and cutting the correct size quick and easy.

CUT DROP

The cut length of fabric. It is the finished length of the curtain or blind, plus top and hem turning allowances.

DOMETT

A soft, fine blanket-like material used as interlining. Thinner than bump. *See also* INTERLINING.

EASE

See TOLERANCE.

EYELET

A two-piece metal ring used for headings on curtains.

EYELET TOOL

A two-part metal hand-setting tool, comprising a round cup and a socket. The back eyelet is placed onto the cup, covered with the fabric from which circles have been cut and the front eyelet is placed on top. These are covered with the socket which is then hammered with a leather-covered mallet to close the eyelets.

FABRIC-COVERED LATH

A pelmet board with a narrow fabric-covered hardboard or ply fascia to conceal the curtain track.

FABRIC-COVERED LEAD PENNY WEIGHTS

Flat, round 2.5cm (1in) diameter lead penny weights, which you cover in lining fabric and place in hems to weigh down the corners.

FABRIC LAMINATION

A fabric laminate is heat-sealed onto furnishing fabric for stiffening and then made up into roller blinds.

FIBREGLASS RODS

Lengths of 4mm (³/₁₆in) diameter fibreglass rod which can be cut to size for inserting into pockets at the back of blinds to support the folds. They will not warp in humid conditions. They will be included in Roman blind kits, or are available separately in 4-metre lengths. Plastic end caps are available to cover the cut ends.

FINIAL

A round or pointed shape, screwed into a curtain pole at both ends to contain the rings.

FINISHED LENGTH

The final length of the blind or curtain when ready to hang.

FLAT BOTTOM BAR

Narrow, flat aluminium bar, usually 2.5cm (1in) in width, used for weighting the hems of Roman blinds to make them hang straight. Will be included in Roman blind kits, or can be bought individually in 3-metre lengths. Plastic end caps are available for the bars to prevent the cut edges snagging the blind.

GATHER HEADING TAPE

A woven tape, with a series of hook loops (known as pockets) and integral draw cords, which is sewn to the top back of curtains. The cords are pulled to form gathers. Hooks are positioned in the pockets, approximately every 10cm (4in) across the gathered curtain. Pockets can be made from straight cords or woven cords, the latter being stronger. Some tapes have several parallel rows of pockets to allow you to adjust the height of your hook positions. Tapes are available in white, natural or translucent. *See also* SMOCK HEADING TAPE.

HEM

The bottom edge of a curtain or blind, which is usually turned under and stitched in place.

HOOK AND LOOP TAPE FASTENER

Also known as Velcro. A fastener consisting of a hooked strip and a looped strip of fabric, which cling together when closed. The loop side is sewn onto fixed-headed curtains and the tops of blinds. The hook side is either stapled onto blind battens and pelmet boards, or pre-glued onto blind headrails. For curtains or blinds use 2cm (³/₄in) in either natural or white. Self-adhesive tape is available, but you would still need to staple or tack it on the hook side. Hook and loop tape fastener can be purchased together or as separate items.

HOOK DROP

The measurement from the eye of the track glider or pole ring to the floor/sill.

HOOK TO HEM

The measurement from the hook to the bottom of the curtain.

HOOK TO TOP

The measurement from the hook to the top of the finished curtain.

INTERLINING

Anything inserted between the face fabric and the lining. *See also* BUMP, DOMETT or BLACK BOLTON TWILL.

LEADING EDGE

The vertical edge of the curtain that will be in the centre of the window when closed.

LINING

A cotton or polycotton sateen-weave fabric. Sewn onto the back of the blind or curtain, it protects the blind or curtain from the sun and improves hanging.

MITRE

A join of two pieces of fabric with their ends tapered so that together they form a right angle. Also used where the hems and side turnings meet.

OVERLAP

Where a pair of curtains cross over in the centre to exclude light and draughts. Allow an extra 7cm (2³⁄₄in) width of fabric.

OVERLONG

Extra length to allow the curtains to lie on the floor. Also referred to as puddling.

PATTERN REPEAT

The length of the pattern on the fabric before it repeats itself.

PELMET BOARD

A piece of planed timber fixed to the wall, like a shelf, used to support a curtain track. Normally 15cm (6in) deep, by 2.5cm (1in).

PIN HOOKS

Small metal hooks that are stabbed into the back of hand-sewn curtain headings.

PIPING

Cord sandwiched inside a strip of fabric and inserted into a seam. Cord should be pre-shrunk cotton or synthetic. For cushions use 3 to 6mm (¹⁄₈–¹⁄₄in) diameter cord.

RAW EDGE

The cut edge of fabric before it has been neatened or hemmed.

RETURN

The space between the front of the curtain and the wall. This is can be covered by the outside edge of the curtain to give a neat finish.

ROD POCKET TAPE

A narrow tube of tape, with integral loops for guiding the blind cords, sewn onto the back of Roman blinds. There are two different types of Roman blind rod pocket tape, which each have two sizes of loops on the front. Single-sew tape is attached to the blind with only one line of machine stitching and has side or end entry holes to insert your rod. Double-sew end entry tape is attached to the blind with two lines of machine stitching and is open at the ends to insert your rod. Sew rings to the tape loops to carry the blind cord or tape, or you can thread your blind cord or tapes through the loops, but this will cause friction and may affect the raising and lowering of your blind. If you intend to thread your cord or tape through the loops, then you must ensure the loops are aligned on each rod pocket so that the cord will be straight.

ROMAN BLIND KIT

Comprising: aluminium headrail with end caps, fibreglass rods with end caps, Roman blind rod pocket tape, 12mm (¹⁄₂in) rings, loop side Velcro, aluminium bottom bar with end caps and universal brackets. A corded kit also includes: cord drop guide, blind cord, cord lock, cord connector, aluminium cord weight with cord drop. The rotary chain kit also includes: tape drops with tape, sidewinder, bead chain and tape-locking clips.

SCREW EYES

A wood screw with an eyelet in place of a head.

SEAM ALLOWANCE

A measurement added to the finished size of your blind, curtain or cushion to allow you to set in your stitch line when sewing fabrics together and create a strong seam.

SELVEDGE

The non-fray woven side edge of the fabric.

SEWING KIT

Comprising: No. 7 long, general hand-sewing needles with long eyes for easy threading, 5cm (2in) glass-headed pins, dressmaker's pins, pin cushion, No. 36 cream and coloured hand-sewing threads, No. 75 machine threads, sewing machine with straight and zigzag stitch, one pair of 24cm (9½in) scissors for cutting fabrics only, one pair of embroidery scissors, one pair of fabric snips, fabric markers, metal 15cm (6in) ruler, retractable steel tape measure, metal-ended fabric tape measure, a clear acrylic set square approximately 40 x 30cm (16 x 12in), metal 1.5m (59in) ruler .

SHEERS

Soft, translucent, gauzy fabrics, such as net, muslin, lace.

SILICON SPRAY

A lubricating aerosol spray made from silicon. Used to make the gliders on curtain tracks and rings on poles run more easily.

SLAT CUTTER

A small plastic guillotine designed to trim plastic or aluminium Venetian blind slats to a bespoke size. It gives a rounded edge to the slat to give a professional finish.

SMOCK HEADING TAPE

A decorative gather heading tape which when drawn up creates a honeycomb effect on the front of the curtain. *See also* GATHER HEADING TAPE.

STACK-BACK

The wall area at the side of the window covered by the curtain. The curtain 'stacks back' or folds into this space when not in use.

STAPLE GUN

A large hand-held gun which will fire 8 to 14mm ($^5/_{16}$–$^9/_{16}$in) staples.

TAPE-LOCKING CLIP

A small plastic clip used to trap the tapes, or cords, on the bottom ring of a Roman blind. The length of tapes, or cords, can be adjusted easily using these clips. There is a range of designs available.

TOLERANCE

An extra measurement added to the finished width of the curtain for ease of movement. Also known as ease.

TRACK

A metal or plastic rail from which curtains are hung.

WINDOW RECESS

The area inside the frame of a window where blinds and sheer curtains can be fitted. Sometimes known as the window reveal.

WOODEN DOWEL

Traditionally used in Roman blinds, 7mm ($^5/_{16}$in) diameter rods are cut to length for inserting into the fabric or lining pockets of Roman blinds to support the folds. They are too wide for most Roman blind rod pocket tapes and are also more prone to warping than fibreglass rods.

VELCRO

See HOOK AND LOOP TAPE FASTENER.

ZIGZAG STITCH

A machined stitch which zigzags from side to side, used to overlock the raw edge of a fabric to prevent fraying.

Merrick & Day curtain books

Everything you need to know about curtains, a range of practical books and patterns for professionals and home sewers alike, a must for every curtain maker's library.

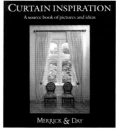

CURTAIN INSPIRATION

Something for everyone – whether your style is country house, urban chic or simple cottage. A full-colour book packed with magnificent photographs to inspire you.

192 pages – 284 x 257mm
295 colour photographs
Hardback ISBN 0 9535267 3 9

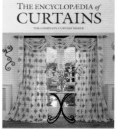

THE ENCYCLOPAEDIA OF CURTAINS

The complete curtain maker's reference book. Easy-to-follow instructions from simple curtains to elaborate swags and tails and pattern cutting. An invaluable how-to book.

240 pages – 300 x 220mm
120 colour photographs
Hardback ISBN 0 9516841 4 0

THE CURTAIN DESIGN DIRECTORY

Design inspiration at a glance – a manual of black-and-white designs for you to identify appropriate window treatments for any situation. A curtain design classic.

320 pages – 284 x 195mm
Over 300 black-and-white drawings
Hardback ISBN 0 9516841 6 7
Ring binder ISBN 0 9516841 9 1

THE FABRIC QUANTITY HANDBOOK

Simple to use for estimating curtain fabric quantities quickly and accurately. Also includes estimation tables for valances, pelmets, swags, blinds, bed valances, covers and much more. Available in either metric or Imperial.

64 pages – 210 x 105mm
43 black-and-white drawings
Metric (yellow hardback) ISBN 0 9516841 7 5
Imperial (red hardback) ISBN 0 9535267 2 0

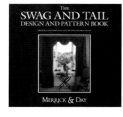

THE SWAG AND TAIL DESIGN BOOK

To make perfect swags and tails every time, choose a design, use the patterns and follow the step-by-step make-up and fitting instructions. Patterns for 60/70/90/120cm wide swags, all in 45cm and 55cm drops, and a range of tail patterns, plus free tissue tracing paper to get started.

104 pages – 250 x 270mm
73 black-and-white drawings, 82 black-and-white diagrams, plus two pattern sheets
Hardback ISBN 0 9516841 8 3

SUPPLEMENTARY SWAG PATTERNS

Additional swag patterns which extend the range of swags in *The Swag and Tail Design and Pattern Book*. The Master Pattern sheets contain full-size swag patterns, 80/100/110/130/140/150/160/170cm wide, all in 45cm and 55cm drops.

Cover – 250 x 270mm
Two pattern sheets (1210 x 1000mm)
Plastic wallet ISBN 0 9535267 0 4

PROFESSIONAL PATTERNS FOR TIE-BACKS

Full-size pattern sheets for plain, banana and scalloped shaped tie-backs, plus make-up instructions. Patterns in eight sizes from 50cm to 120cm embraces.

Cover – 250 x 270mm
Three pattern sheets (500 x 700mm)
Plastic wallet ISBN 0 9516841 3 2

SOFT FURNISHING MASTER SYSTEM

Invaluable forms for all, whether your business is large or small. From measuring sheets for a range of window shapes to make-up sheets for all types of window treatments. Photocopy the appropriate form and fill in as required.

70 loose-leaf pages
Ring binder ISBN 0 9535267 1 2

Mail order curtain-making products
from Merrick & Day

If you're now feeling inspired to start making your own blinds, curtains and cushions, then take a look at our website **www.merrick-day.com** or phone **08707 570980** for a brochure.

We stock everything you need to make beautiful soft furnishings; from Roman blind kits, blind components, buckrams, heading tapes, hooks and rings, linings and interlinings, workroom tools, tracks and poles, brassware, to cushion pads and zips. In fact, everything except the fabric!

We have carefully selected our wide range of sundries and products for their quality and cost-effectiveness, so you can buy with confidence. Many of the items are used regularly in our workroom.

We offer direct prices for cut lengths and small quantities and trade prices for full rolls and trade quantities.

We can usually deliver next day in the UK, 2–3 days for Highlands and Islands. Contact us for details.

Curtain-making courses
with Merrick & Day

Inspirational one-day courses offering expert tuition within the personal yet professional atmosphere of the Merrick & Day North Lincolnshire workroom.

Gain confidence, share the enjoyment of, and experience first-hand, expert curtain making and all that it entails.

All courses are suitable for intermediate and advanced curtain makers as well as those new to the craft.

One-day courses include:
Designing window treatments, measuring windows, interlined curtains, interlined valances, flat pelmets, Roman blinds, advanced Roman blinds, swags and tails, swag valances and arched windows.

Intensive three-day curtain design and make-up courses are available for experienced sewers, covering all aspects of curtain making. Contact us for dates and availability.

Index

Picture credits

We would like to thank all the companies who have generously allowed us to use their photographs in this book, and also thanks to the interior designers who have kindly allowed us to photograph their work. Without their support, this book would not have been possible.

VANESSA ARBUTHNOTT – Fabrics
T: 01285 831437, www.vanessaarbuthnott.co.uk
Page 31, Woodland; page 46, Feather & Egg, Chicken Check.

SALLY DERNIE – Interior design
T: 020 7738 1628, www.sallydernie.com
Page 37.

CAROUSEL DESIGN – Interior design
T: 020 7794 3116, www.carouseldesign.co.uk
Pages 28 & 29.

SUE DYSON – Interior design
T: 020 7460 9537
Pages 10 & 11.

HARLEQUIN – Fabrics
Retail enquiries - T: 08708 300032
HJH Showroom, Chelsea Harbour Design Centre, London SW10 0XE, UK
Trade enquiries - T: 08708 300355
Ladybird House, Beeches Road, Loughborough, Leicestershire LE11 2HA, UK
www.harlequin.uk.com

Front cover, right, Orient; back cover, Odyssey; page 2, Mendhi; page 5, centre, Eden, bottom, Orient; page 6, Linen voiles; page 30, Fleur; page 68, Eden; page 69, Mendhi; pages 70–1, Orient; page 72, Linen voiles; page 73, Eden; page 74, Mendhi; page 75, Odyssey; page 76, left, Mendhi, right, Picardy weaves; page 77, Mendhi; pages 84–5, Odyssey; page 86, Orient; page 87, Picardy weaves; page 111, Orient; page 114, Orient; pages 116–18, Mendhi; pages 119–20, Orient; page 121, Picardy weaves; page 122, Fleur; page 123, Picardy weaves; page 126, Orient; page 127, Odyssey; page 129, Honesty; page 130, Mendhi; page 131, Orient; page 132, Eden; page 133, top, Odyssey, bottom, Picardy weaves.

CAROLYN HOLMES INTERIORS – Interior design
T: 01235 848480, www.carolynholmesinteriors.com
Page 5, top; page 8; page 14; page 38; page 39.

LOUVOLITE – Blinds
Ashton Road, Hyde, Cheshire SK14 4BG, UK
T: 0161 882 5000, www.louvolite.com

Page 12, Dominica; page 16, Birch; page 17, Snowberry; page 18 Montana Moccasin; page 19 Montana; page 20, Bali Black; page 21, Carnival White; page 22, Martinique Natural; page 23 Martinique and Antigua Natural; page 24, Crush Apple; page 25, Crush Caramel; page 27, Manhattan Madison.

JILL SCHOLES – Interior design
T: 020 8969 7001, www.jillscholes.co.uk
Page 8; page 34; page 83.

THE TREEHOUSE INTERIORS – Interior design
T: 01522 823506, www.thetreehouseinteriors.com
Page 33; page 78; page 88.

WALCOT HOUSE – Poles, clips and eyeleting service
T: 01993 832940, www.walcothouse.co.uk

Page 80, leather tabs on Lincoln cream; page 81, silver spring clip on Lincoln yellow; page 82, black eyelet on Hanover navy; page 104, twisted spring clips on Lincoln blue; page 105, leather tabs on Lincoln yellow.

Merrick & Day photographs taken by Mike Beard.